More Praise for *The Essentials of Business Etiquette*

"Barbara has once again written an excellent and timely compendium of stories, tips, and strategies that are invaluable for both new entrants in business as well as older professionals who need to brush up and update their business etiquette skills to meet the new demands of our society. A wonderful, fun, and easy read!"

—Molly D. Shepard, MS, MSM, President and CEO,
The Leader's Edge/Leader's By Design

"Being aware of your personal brand is a conscious effort. *The Essentials of Business Etiquette* offers clear, relevant advice on the 'smart' way to build and maintain your brand. It also reminds us that how you present yourself can be the differentiator in your success."

—Maureen Duffy, Vice President, Corporate Communications
and External Affairs, American Water

"Barbara Pachter offers indispensable advice to professionals at every level in their careers—from new graduates to CEOs."

—Laura Stern, President, Nautilus Solar Energy, LLC

"Full of relevant, up-to-date information, *The Essentials of Business Etiquette* helps readers effectively navigate the complex, ever-changing world of social media. Through real-life examples and stories, Barbara Pachter provides valuable insight into the best ways to leverage your skills for professional advantage."

—Teressa Moore Griffin, speaker, coach,
and author of *LIES That Limit*

"Barbara Pachter has once again written a very commonsense and easy-to-read book to help executives and college students alike. Whether the reader is looking for keys to advance in his or her career or looking for that first job after graduation, this book has something for everyone. "

—Thomas W. Sidlik, Board of Directors Member,
Delphi Automotive PLC, Chairman Emeritus,
Eastern Michigan University

Other Books by Barbara Pachter

New Rules @ Work: 79 Etiquette Tips, Tools,
and Techniques to Get Ahead and Stay Ahead

When the Little Things Count . . .
and They Always Count

The Jerk with the Cell Phone:
A Survival Guide for the Rest of Us

The Power of Positive Confrontation:
The Skills You Need to Know to Handle Conflicts
at Work, at Home, and in Life

Minding Your Business Manners

Prentice Hall Complete Business Etiquette Handbook

Business Etiquette

Climbing the Corporate Ladder:
What You Need to Know and Do
to Be a Promotable Person

THE ESSENTIALS

═══ OF ═══

BUSINESS
ETIQUETTE

HOW TO GREET, EAT, AND
TWEET YOUR WAY TO SUCCESS

Barbara Pachter

with Denise Cowie

New York   Chicago   San Francisco   Athens   London   Madrid   Mexico City
Milan   New Delhi   Singapore   Sydney   Toronto

9 10 DOC 19 18 17 16

ISBN 978-0-07-181126-2
MHID 0-07-181126-5

e-ISBN 978-0-07-181127-9
e-MHID 0-07-181127-3

Library of Congress Cataloging-in-Publication Data

Pachter, Barbara.
  The essentials of business etiquette : how to greet, eat, and tweet your way to success / by Barbara Pachter.
      pages cm
  Includes bibliographical references.
  ISBN-13: 978-0-07-181126-2 (alk. paper)
  ISBN-10: 0-07-181126-5 (alk. paper)
  1. Business ethics. I. Title.
  HF5387.P333 2013
  395.5'2—dc23
                                                          2013002469

McGraw-Hill Education books are available at special quantity discounts to use as premiums and sales promotions or for use in corporate training programs. To contact a representative, please visit the Contact Us pages at www.mhprofessional.com.

This book is printed on acid-free paper.

For the next generation of business professionals:

Connor, Blake, Logan, and Gavin
Poppy, Annabella Drew, and Pelton

Contents

PART 2. MAINTAINING A PROFESSIONAL IMAGE

SECTION II. EAT

SECTION III. TWEET

SECTION IV. CAREER

Introduction

"Your career is what you make it."

How many times have you heard that line? It's an easy statement to make, but a harder reality to implement—unless you cultivate the skills to do so.

For the last 25 years, I have given seminars, coached individuals, and written nine books on business etiquette and communication. They all discuss specific skills to help people understand how they should present themselves in the workplace to advance in their careers. My clients include some of the world's leading companies, such as Campbell's Soup, Chrysler, Cleveland Clinic, Con Edison, Microsoft, Pfizer, and Wawa. I generally give about a hundred presentations a year to employees at all levels.

Several years ago, I started a blog. This informal platform allows me to discuss or comment on the most up-to-date ideas and recommendations as they evolve from today's business world. Focusing on real-life examples, my blogs discuss what I have learned from people at all levels of business, from presidents of companies to young people starting out in their careers.

This book is a compilation of my favorite blogs, current writings, and new essential tips chosen for their informative content and practical recommendations. The businesspeople I work with every day like the timely commentary and suggestions the blog delivers, and many of them asked me to create an easy-to-read business etiquette guide for quick reference. Thanks to the encouragement of Casie Vogel at McGraw-Hill Professional, this book, written in collaboration with Denise Cowie, my writing and editing buddy of many years, is now a reality.

The topics I discuss are rarely covered in business schools, but they will help you to establish relationships easily, dress professionally, use social media successfully, speak assertively, write confidently, entertain effortlessly, look for work effectively, and make presentations competently. The suggestions are geared to your business life, but of course many of the ideas can help in your personal life too.

The book is divided into four sections and has 101 entries. I recommend that you read just a few at a time, or find suggestions for a specific problem by checking the Contents. Think about the material carefully—pay attention to the points made, and consider whether you really are following the advice.

In addition to reading the tips, experiment with some of the ideas in the "Try This Suggestion" sections, learn from the question-and-answer sections, and consider the "Points to Ponder."

Don't dismiss a topic as not relevant to you until you have evaluated how the content might help you improve your work skills—or your social life. It is easy *not* to know you are doing something when you have been doing it for a long time. As one senior vice president from a Fortune 100 company told me:

Time after time, I find that very competent managers and executives are totally unaware of their self-inflicted career-limiting behavior.

Barbara Pachter

== SECTION I ==

GREET

- *A senior director for a major pharmaceutical company was scheduled to start traveling the world for his company. But his ill-fitting, rumpled clothes and casual language would be an embarrassment for his company overseas. His superiors decided he needed to acquire some polish before he could represent the company.*
- *A representative for a management company sought a contract to manage a physical therapy business. The owners of the business deliberately left her for a while in the common waiting area so they could evaluate her interactions with patients and office staff. The woman did not talk to anyone in the waiting area, and she did not smile or greet any of the patients. She did not get the contract.*

These real-life examples illustrate the need for business etiquette training. These individuals needed to improve their efforts to connect with others or to enhance their professional image to be successful—or more successful—in their jobs.

Just doing your job in our competitive, global business environment isn't enough. You need to stand out—in a good way. You want others to see you as a competent, credible, and responsive individual.

I

And that means that you need to connect with others, and you also need to have a polished, professional appearance.

Your ability to get along with people, to exhibit good manners, to project an impressive image, and to make others feel comfortable are key components of your success. In today's fast-paced, digital, multicultural world, these business etiquette skills can sometimes get lost in the shuffle. But without them, your organization may lose business, your colleagues may lose respect for you, and your bosses may not promote you.

There are two parts that make up Section I, "Greet": "Establishing Rapport" (Part 1) and "Maintaining a Professional Image" (Part 2).

ESTABLISHING RAPPORT

A major area of business etiquette is establishing rapport. This is an incredibly important part of most people's jobs, though it's rarely listed on their job descriptions.

You want to connect with others. You *need* to connect with others. Why? Because people want to do business and work with those they know, like, and trust.

Sounds simple, right? It can be, if you remember to practice the basics for establishing rapport—greeting and acknowledging others, and conducting conversations effectively and politely.

1. What's in Your Name? A Lot!

Names are important. How people address you and what you call yourself really do matter. Names can confer dignity or take it away. They influence how you are perceived and whether people take you seriously.

In a business situation, you should use your full name. An intern working for me answered the phone by saying: "Good morning. Pachter & Associates. Brianna speaking."

I asked why she used just her first name. She said she hadn't realized she was doing it. I suggested she provide both her first and last names. That would not only give her standing but would also provide an easier way for people to identify her. After all, there could be other people in the office with the same first name.

POINT TO PONDER

Early on, basketball legend Michael Jordan recognized the value of a name. The television news magazine *60 Minutes* did a segment a few years ago on the famous athlete's history, including the time he scored, as a first-year college student, the winning basket in the 1982 National Collegiate Athletic Association (NCAA) championship game. According to the reporter, that's when he went from being called "Mike Jordan" to "Michael Jordan."

The flip side of using your full name is knowing how to address others. Etiquette says you should call people what they want to be called:

- Pay attention when people introduce themselves, or notice what they write on their name tags. They are giving you information about how they would like to be addressed.

- Don't shorten someone's name or use a nickname unless you know the person wants it that way. A man in one of my seminars said that his name was Roberto. If someone called him "Robert," he would not respond.

- If you don't know what to call a business associate, you can always ask.

TRY THIS SUGGESTION

Name tags often are used at meetings and conferences to identify people. Place your name tag on your right-hand side, slightly below the shoulder. This makes it more visible when you are shaking hands.

Q. *My last name is very difficult for people to pronounce, and they get frustrated trying to say it correctly. Should I change my name?*

A. If people have stopped addressing you because they can't pronounce your name—which is usually not done out of malice but embarrassment—one solution is, as you suggest, a name change. But changing your name is a very personal, often difficult decision. An alternative is to let people know to call you by your first name and to hand them your business card showing the proper spelling of your last name for any correspondence.

If your first name is difficult, you could create an easy-to-pronounce diminutive version for common use. One man I encountered had a first name that was 11 letters long. He did shorten his name, and he has never regretted it.

2. The Name Game: And You Are . . . ?

It seems so obvious, but it's surprising how often people fail to do this: *Remember to introduce yourself after someone has introduced himself or herself to you.*

This may seem like a little thing, but it's important.

Let me explain. Before most of my seminars begin, I shake hands with each participant and say, "Hi, I'm Barbara Pachter, your instructor. Welcome, and enjoy the day." Many people respond appropriately and introduce themselves to me.

This etiquette give-and-take paves the way for a connection between the two people and makes it easier for conversation to begin.

Yet, there are some participants who don't give their names. They just shake hands, or they shake hands and only say "Hi." An awkward silence usually follows. This means that I will often jump in and politely ask, "And you are . . . ?"

When people don't volunteer their names without prompting, they can appear shy, timid, or standoffish. As a result, making a connection or starting a conversation can be more difficult.

It's not just in my seminars that people fail to give their names. People tell me the same thing happens to them when they attend meetings and introduce themselves to the men or women sitting next to them.

Why do people do this?

In my classes, I know that some people simply are startled. They are not expecting the instructor to practice this protocol. A woman recently sent me a thank you note emphasizing how much she enjoyed meeting me before the seminar started. She hadn't experienced this with other instructors. In other situations, some people don't give their names because they are preoccupied, and others just don't know that they should do so.

TRY THIS SUGGESTION

Monitor your own behavior. Pay attention when people introduce themselves, and—please!—respond with your full name.

3. Impressive Introductions

In the business world, people often find themselves in situations in which introductions are required. Who should take on this task? Many times it will be your responsibility. If you are the host, the person in charge, or you know both parties, you need to make the introductions.

These days, the name of the person of highest rank is said first, regardless of gender. For example, "Mr. Greater Importance, I would like you to meet Ms. Lesser Importance." Don't drive yourself crazy trying to determine who is more important. If you don't know, mention first the name of the person that you would like to flatter. The key is that the introduction needs to take place.

You could also add some information about each person to encourage conversation. For example:

Brittany Miller, this is Jennifer Cortez. Jennifer just joined us as a new sales representative. Brittany is the manager of sales training.

POINT TO PONDER

People often won't notice whether their name was said first or last. They will remember—and potentially hold it against you—if your lack of introductions made them feel uncomfortable, regardless of whether this happens in a business or a social setting. As one seminar participant told me:

My ex-boyfriend would never introduce me, but he finally got the point when I started saying, "Hi. I'm Jenny. I'll introduce myself because I know he won't do it." His lack of introduction always made me feel awkward and insignificant.

(Note that she did refer to him as her ex-boyfriend.)

Occasionally, if you are the stranger in the room, you may need to introduce yourself. This self-introduction should be planned and practiced, but it also should be tailored to the event. Keep it short, but provide enough information to help start the conversation. For example, "I'm Brian Corbett, the tax expert on today's program. It's a pleasure to meet you."

Q. *Last week I entered the elevator, and the president of my company was already there. We were the only two people, but I just said "Hi." Should I have said more?*

A. You can greet the person (which you did), but you also can introduce yourself. If you can, open a dialogue. Make a brief self-reveal statement ("I'm part of the new marketing team, and I look forward to working here"), or make an observation ("I see you have a new iPad; I just got one and really like it"). If he responds with more than a nod, you can continue the conversation. If he seems preoccupied, you can feel good that you said "Hello." Make sure you say goodbye, and use an exit line when you leave the elevator ("Bye. Have a good day.").

---

4. I'd Like You to Meet . . . Er . . . Um . . .

I was so embarrassed. I forgot my colleague's name when I went to introduce him to my boss. I just wasn't expecting to see him at the meeting.

This kind of comment from a seminar participant is one I get a lot. What do you do if you start to introduce someone to another person but realize midintroduction that you've forgotten his or her name?

You admit it. Everyone forgets a name occasionally, and some of us more often than that—which is why you should have some standard lines ready:

- "I'm sorry, I've forgotten your name."

- "Your face is so familiar; I just can't recall your name."

- "My mental computer is down. I can't access your name."

- "My mind has gone blank. What is your name?"

Keep it short and sweet, and practice saying it until you feel you can deliver the line without excessive apology or embarrassment. That should get you through a difficult moment.

This is a technique I call *Know Your Line*—knowing in advance what you might say in an awkward situation instead of being at a loss for words. If you have practiced what you want to say until you are comfortable saying it, people are more likely to be comfortable when hearing it.

It's also a useful technique for getting through some of those discomfiting conversational moments that crop up all too often. For example, one woman who was very tall often had people approach her and say, rather thoughtlessly, "Boy, are you tall!" She wanted a rejoinder, a line without curse words in it. Her line became: "Yes, I can paint without a ladder!"

POINT TO PONDER

Should you ever try to bluff your way through when you realize you've forgotten the name of somebody you have to introduce? Maybe—but be aware of the risks. You can say, "Have you two met each other?" and hope the answer is affirmative. But if both people respond "No," you'll find yourself in the middle of a very awkward situation.

5. Sorry, Mom: *Do* Talk to Strangers

It's [Taylor Swift's] tireless courting of her fans that may be the key to her success. Remarkably, she spends an hour before every show meeting and greeting and charming. —Lesley Stahl, *60 Minutes*

No doubt your mother told you not to talk to strangers. That is good advice for children—but it doesn't apply in the business world. Say "Hello," "Good morning," or simply "Hi" to people you know, *and* to those you don't know. You really don't need to know someone to say "Hello" to him or her. (Clearly, different rules apply in dark alleys!)

The person you greet on the way to the meeting may be the person sitting next to you at the meeting, and by saying "Hello," you've already established minor rapport. You will more likely be viewed as an approachable, friendly person. And who doesn't want to work with people who connect with them?

POINT TO PONDER

Consider this feedback from a job applicant: "I was told that I got my position because the front-desk folks thought that I was friendly and very welcoming and the other candidates were not. The two receptionists said the CEO always asks for their opinion."

People assume they practice this very basic courtesy of greeting others, but if everybody really were doing so, I wouldn't keep hearing this comment: "I walk around corporate America, and no one says anything!" So I ask you, who is doing the greeting?

Also be mindful of what greetings you use because not all greetings are equally acceptable and people can get offended. I was asked to coach a man who used "Howdy" when he greeted his customers.

One of his customers called the vice president to complain that he was acting "too casual" with him.

"Yo!" is not a corporate greeting. Say "Hi" or "Hello" instead. You may hear people greeting others with "Hey!" at work, but this really is too informal for most business situations.

Be aware of your own behavior. Make sure you are greeting and acknowledging others. And if someone says "Hello" to you, you *must* say "Hello" back. It's not optional. People often tell me that when they do start saying "Hello," people sometimes don't respond. That is just rude—but not everyone realizes that.

POINTS TO PONDER

1. A bleary-eyed salesperson didn't feel much like talking to anyone when he climbed on the treadmill early in the morning at his conference's hotel gym, but he greeted the man on the machine next to him, anyway, and they spoke for a few minutes. Later in the day, he discovered that his treadmill buddy was the key person he wanted to see at the conference. His good manners had an unexpected payoff—the man was glad to see him again, and they ultimately did business.

2. The janitor was still doing a final tidy-up in the conference room when his company's sales representatives arrived for their quarterly meeting. Eventually, the regional manager opened the session: "Let's get started, although the president who is going to address us isn't here yet." At this point, the janitor pulled off his cap and coverall to reveal a business suit. "Oh, yes, he is," said the disguised president, "and the first point I want to make is that only three people in this entire room greeted a fellow employee—the janitor. Everyone else ignored an opportunity to make a connection. And you call yourselves salespeople!"

6. Kissing Colleagues: Is It Ever Okay?

I greeted a job candidate, and he grabbed me by the shoulders and kissed me on the lips. Aack! We are always looking for auditors who are quick thinkers and show initiative, but this was a bit much. The kissing bandit didn't get the job.

That tale from a financial manager involved with hiring illustrates one of the many downsides to kissing in the workplace: if you greet someone inappropriately, you may lose a job or a work opportunity. You may also come across as a little strange!

Greeting someone with a kiss on the cheek when others are around also may cause difficulty. (An attractive salesperson greeted one of her customers at a business dinner with such a kiss—unfortunately, right in front of his disapproving wife.) Plus, others observing the kiss might assume that it is acceptable for them to greet the person in a similar manner, which would most likely not be the case. However, the main reason to avoid this kind of behavior is that the man or woman you greet with a kiss may be very uncomfortable with the greeting.

The handshake is *the* business greeting in the U.S. workplace, and I strongly encourage both men and women to shake hands. Nevertheless, when discussing greetings in my etiquette seminars, I am often asked, "Is it ever okay to greet someone with a kiss?" The answer is a cautious "Yes, but . . ."

Businesspeople need to consider the following before puckering up:

1. **Their relationship with the other person.** When people know each other well, they may kiss or hug even in business settings. But people still need to remember the drawbacks and use common sense—a young woman greets her long-time mentor with a kiss

in his office, but she wisely shakes his hand when greeting him at meetings. It is unwise to greet a stranger or casual acquaintance with a kiss.

2. **The type of company for which they work.** Kissing as a greeting occurs less in large and/or conservative companies than in smaller, creative or informal offices.

3. **The nationality of the other person.** People from other countries doing business in the United States might greet business associates with their traditional greeting—possibly a kiss on one or both cheeks. They may know that in the United States, businesspeople usually shake hands, but they inadvertently use their home country's greeting. In such a case, good manners suggest that you participate in the greeting to put the visitor at ease.

And when in doubt, shake hands. In the U. S. business world, shaking hands is the default greeting.

7. The Thumb Joint Connects to the . . .
Thumb Joint

*The manager didn't extend his hand. I didn't know whether
to extend my hand or not.*

There's often some confusion about who initiates the handshake,
as this comment I heard from a new hire indicates. Yes, she should
have. In today's workplace, the higher-ranking person or the host,
regardless of gender, should extend his or her hand first. But if the
higher-ranking person fails to do so immediately—often because of
the gender confusion—the lower-ranking person should extend his
or her hand without missing more than a beat.

The key is that the handshake must take place. I cannot emphasize this enough. In the United States, the handshake is the business
greeting. If you want to be taken seriously, you must shake hands and
shake hands correctly.

Even if we aren't aware of doing so, we make assumptions about
people based on the quality of their handshake. If someone gives you
a limp handshake, what do you think? Be honest. Yes, your immediate
impression is that the person is weak.

When you shake hands, you should extend your hand with the
thumb up. Touch thumb joint to thumb joint. Put your thumb down,
and wrap your fingers around the palm of the other person. Your
grip should be firm, but don't break any bones—it's not a competition. Two to three pumps is enough. Face the person, and make eye
contact as well.

These days, both men and women should stand when being introduced or when greeting others. Many people believe they do, even
though they don't. I often introduce myself to individual participants

before beginning my seminars, and whenever someone fails to stand for the introduction, I tell that participant to remember the word *Facebook*. Later, I ask the entire group if they stand when shaking hands. Almost all of them say, "Yes." Then I continue: "If I told you to remember the word *Facebook*, you did *not* stand." Many are shocked at their own behavior.

Standing helps establish your presence. You make it easy for others to ignore you if you don't stand. If you are caught off guard and cannot rise, you should lean forward to indicate that you would stand, if you could.

TRY THIS SUGGESTION

What do people think about your handshake? It's important to know.

Practice with a trusted colleague. Start by shaking hands just gripping each other's fingers, then gripping knuckles, and finally thumb joint to thumb joint. The last position is, of course, the correct one. Ask your practice buddy whether your squeeze is firm but not hurtful. By practicing how this handshake feels, you will be able to recognize that you are doing it correctly with business associates.

POINT TO PONDER

Keep the right hand free. Before you walk into a meeting, move anything you are carrying to your left hand. You don't want to be fumbling with items before you extend your hand. When mingling, hold your drink in the left hand so your right hand is always free and dry to shake.

8. But . . . I Have More Questions About the Handshake

The handshake can be big news. Consider these headlines:

French World Cup Coach Refuses Handshake with South Africa's Coach

Bush Wipes Hand on Clinton's Shirt After Shaking Hands in Haiti

Obama Fist-Bump Rocks the Nation!

Headlines like those may be part of the reason I get so many questions about the handshake—from both seasoned professionals and new hires. Many of them haven't been taught the ins and outs of the handshake. It's not usually part of a college curriculum.

We've covered the major points you need to know to master a businesslike handshake, but students in my seminars and readers of my blog often come up with other concerns, such as the following:

Q. *What do you do if you can't shake hands?*
A. One woman emailed that she doesn't want to shake hands because she has arthritis in her hands. She explained, "I am reentering the job market after a period of retirement, and I'm wondering how I can gracefully discourage handshaking." I suggested that she smile and say something like, "My arthritis is acting up; I'm sorry, but I'm unable to shake hands."

Q. *Is it okay to use the fist-bump in the corporate world?*
A. The handshake is still the business greeting in the United States, and people expect a handshake. I also think that with a fist-bump attempt, it's too easy to miss the other person's fist.

Q. *I am worried about germs. Do I have to greet people with a handshake?*

A. The answer is similar to the one above: people are expecting you to shake their hands, and if you don't, you are cutting yourself off from them. If you are really concerned about shaking someone's hand, shake his or her hand anyway, and then find a reason to excuse yourself and go wash your hands. Or find a private moment to use a hand sanitizer discreetly.

Q. *Is it appropriate for the other person to place his or her thumb on top of mine?*

A. No. This is not thumb wrestling. Both parties extend their hands with the thumb up, touch thumb joint to thumb joint, and bend their thumbs down as they grip. This way, neither thumb is on top of the other.

Q. *What do you do if the other person has a bone-crushing grip?*

A. Let your hand go limp. It's a self-defense technique, and many times your hand can slide through. Also, if you know you are going to be in a position of shaking hands a lot, remove any rings from your right hand—because if someone squeezes your hand when you have rings on, it can really hurt.

Q. *What happens if I extend my hand and the other person doesn't respond?*

A. Just put your hand down. Your behavior is correct. But this question does bring up some additional handshake concerns:

- **Cultural.** Among certain followers of Orthodox Judaism, Islam, and possibly others, men are not allowed to touch women who are not their spouses. If that is the case, it is really that person's responsibility to politely say something like, "Oh, I'm so sorry. I'm unable to shake hands." This situation can be confusing. One Muslim woman told me that at work she will shake hands with men, but at home she doesn't. When I was teaching in the Middle East, occasionally one of my students would cover his hand with his sleeve before we shook hands so we weren't touching flesh to flesh.

- **Disabilities.** If you know the person isn't able to shake hands, don't extend your hand. If you don't know for sure, extend your hand—this way, you are including the person. It is then that person's responsibility to say something like, "Oh, I'm so sorry. I'm unable to shake hands." One man I encountered said, "I don't shake. My dog does it for me." The dog then extended his paw.

9. Business Cards in a Social-Media World

I recently gave my business card to a potential client. She was impressed that my Facebook address (www.facebook.com/pachtertraining) was on my card because she had seen few cards where small business owners provided that information.

Business cards tell people what you do, and they provide a way for them to contact you. Because social media have changed the way we connect with our customers, clients, colleagues, and employers, your card may need to include additional information—such as your addresses for Facebook, LinkedIn, Twitter, or your blog. You will have to decide how much to include and how to do so without overloading your card.

To help you make this decision, ask yourself these questions:

1. **Have I included the necessary information?** Think about the majority of your potential clients and customers, and include on the card the information they will need. This usually means your name, your title, company name and/or logo, address, phone number, and email and web addresses.

2. **What can I eliminate?** Is the information on the card easy to read? Make sure your card is visually appealing—that means it should not look cramped or crowded. Can you eliminate your fax number? Do you need both your business and cell phone numbers? If you have a lot of information you must include, use the back for the less essential information.

3. **Which social-media addresses do I use for business?** Include the social-media addresses that help you stay in contact with your customers, clients, and other business associates. If adding all your links overwhelms the card, place them on the back. When

you hand your card to someone, you can point this out by saying, "If you want to connect with me by social media, my addresses are on the back."

4. **Should I include a Quick Response (QR) code?** QR codes are bar codes that can be scanned by smartphones to provide a link to your websites or LinkedIn profile. If you include a QR code, generally you would place it on the back of the card.

5. **Is a photograph necessary?** Most corporate cards do not include photographs, but you may want to include a photograph if you use your card for marketing purposes. Speakers will often have photographs of themselves on their cards.

If you want to give someone your card, and the person has not asked for it, ask that person for his or hers. This makes it much easier to add, "Oh, and here is mine."

TRY THIS SUGGESTION

Keep your business cards readily available and in good shape. If you are attending a networking function, make sure you have a system for keeping incoming and outgoing cards separate, such as putting the cards you are giving out in one pocket and the cards you are receiving in another pocket.

10. Small Talk, Big Talk, and Everything in Between

Two managers were competing for a promotion. Both were professionally competent. Yet, only one of them had outstanding social skills. She was the one who could strike up a conversation with anyone. She appeared outgoing and interesting. The other manager avoided events. She often stood by herself and hated making small talk.

Who was picked for the promotion? The confident socializer, of course.

Some people, like the affable manager described above, are born with the gift of gab, and they find it easy to talk to anyone. It's truly an art. And we love these people, especially when we're hosting a party. But for the rest of us, conversation can be more like a science—which means there are skills to learn to make conversation. The good news is that we can all acquire these skills if we are willing to do some preparation:

- **Look the person up on LinkedIn.** If you know you are going to be meeting with a specific person, get to know a little bit about that person's background. Look the individual up on social-media sites such as LinkedIn to find out about his or her interests and achievements.

- **Arm yourself for conversation.** To prepare, you need topics and materials to discuss. Read news sites on the Internet, your daily newspapers, and newsmagazines that are likely to cover broad topics in digest form. Watch news shows like *60 Minutes*, *20/20*, or *Dateline*.

Read your professional journals. They provide up-to-date in-formation about your profession.

You also need to observe the world around you. On the way to a meeting, did you pass a billboard announcing a concert or sporting event? Is there new construction right next door to your meeting venue? This kind of information can provide good mate-rial for conversation.

- **Use "safe" topics.** You can talk about the weather (front-page stories such as hurricanes generally have more appeal), traffic, common experiences, travel, entertainment (movies, plays), holiday celebra-tions, upbeat business news, vacations, current events (cautiously), and the activity you are attending.

  If everyone in the conversational group is interested, you can talk about sports. Again, front-page sports, such as the Olympics, have a wider appeal.

  You can talk about family, if others in the conversation share a common interest. Discussing your child's soccer experiences with a client who also has a child playing soccer can be a great way to connect with him or her.

  Make sure to stay away from talk about sex, politics, and religion. Let me say that again: *stay away from sex, politics, and religion.* People may hold views that differ greatly from yours. And discovering this can cause people to change their opinions of others, usually to their detriment. (See Etiquette 15, "Political Discussions to Avoid at Work.")

  Other topics to avoid are your health, what things cost, gossip, and off-color jokes.

Q. *In your seminars you have said, "Constant complaining about your company or the economy or anything else is a downer." Why is it important to keep the conversation upbeat?*

A. You want to appear as an upbeat, positive, can-do type of person. Why would I want to work with or hire someone who is negative? Negative people can have a "Why bother?" attitude—why bother to try to fix things or make them better? Plus, it's depressing to listen to people discuss negative things all the time.

11. Go Ahead—Meet New People

One etiquette-related complaint I hear repeatedly from my clients is that when their employees attend business social events such as conferences and association meetings, they talk only to a small group of people from within their own company. They ignore the opportunity to meet new people—potential new customers!

At an association meeting I attended, I saw employees from one company sitting together. After talking to them for a few minutes, I asked why they weren't mingling. One woman confessed that she didn't like initiating conversation with people she didn't know. She said that once the conversation was under way, she was fine—it was just getting started that bothered her.

I gave her the following ideas. Try them out at your next networking event. You don't want to miss opportunities to expand your network or to meet potential clients or possible future employers.

- **Pretend you are the host of an event**. Now, it is your job to make others feel comfortable. This forces you to focus on other people, not on yourself. You will be amazed at how successful you will be when you play this mind game.

- **Go up to a person who is alone.** Most people are grateful for the company. Say hello, introduce yourself, and shake hands. Ask the person a question, and listen to what the person has to say. If he or she seems uninterested, excuse yourself and move on to the next person.

- **Talk to the people next to you while in line for food or drink**. Make eye contact, smile, and express a positive comment about the food, the surroundings, or the event. If the person responds, you are into a conversation. I did this at an event recently, and I ended up with a new client as a result.

- **When you first sit down at a meeting, turn to the people on either side of you.** Say hello, and introduce yourself. This usually leads to conversation.

TRY THIS SUGGESTION

You can encourage more conversation with comments like these: "Tell me more; it sounds as if you had a great time," or "What an interesting situation; what else happened?" Self-revealing statements like "I know what you mean; I was in a similar situation last year" can also add to the discussion.

- **Join larger groups.** If two people are talking to each other, they may be having a private conversation. It could be awkward to approach them. Larger groups are usually engaged in generalized conversation. You can casually join such a group, listen for a while, and when appropriate, you can add to the conversation.

POINT TO PONDER

During a discussion about the benefits of initiating conversation, a seminar participant stressed that I was absolutely correct. She said that she usually didn't talk to strangers, especially on planes, but on one flight she had forgotten her Kindle, so she spoke to the man next to her. He was very pleasant, and they talked throughout the three-hour trip.

Two hours into the conversation, she found out that he was the CEO of a company she had been trying to meet with for months. She ended her story with a big smile and added, "My meeting with his company is in two weeks!"

Her decision to connect with a stranger not only made a flight more pleasant but also paid off handsomely down the line. I later discovered that as a result of the meeting, she got the company's business.

12. Opening Lines . . . in the Air and Elsewhere

Shortly after I took my seat on a Southwest Airlines flight, the woman next to me began eating the food she had brought on board. I said to her, "I have been a vegetarian for 20 years, but I have to tell you, your hamburger smells delicious!" She laughed, and we started to talk.

During our conversation, she asked if I would like some airline coupons for free drinks, as she had extras. I accepted—what a nice benefit from talking to your seatmate.

As I was enjoying my glass of wine, I looked closely at the remaining coupons and realized that printed on them were tips on how to start a conversation. That made my day! Since I teach etiquette, I am always pleased when companies provide suggestions.

Southwest's "Conversation Starters" were questions you could ask the person sitting next to you, such as "When was the first time you flew Southwest Airlines? Where did you go?"

In addition to questions like those, try the following suggestions as well. These examples can be used on planes . . . and just about everywhere else:

- **Make a self-revelation.** My statement about being a vegetarian was an example of a self-revelation. Keep all comments relevant and positive.

- **Comment on your surroundings.** "I just read that book. It's great—and I promise I won't tell you the ending."

- **Give a sincere compliment.** "That's a gorgeous coat. Did you buy it on your trip?"

- **Avoid closed-ended questions.** These are questions that can be answered with yes or no. Open-ended questions demand longer answers, which gives you more opportunity to extend the conversation. Instead of "Did you have a difficult time in traffic today?" for example, ask, "How did you manage with traffic today?"

The more you practice implementing these etiquette suggestions, the easier they become.

THE GOLDEN RULE OF MAKING CONVERSATION: LISTEN!

> The reason you don't understand me, Edith, is because I'm talking to you in English and you're listening to me in dingbat.
> —Archie Bunker in *All in the Family*

We live in a world where people always seem to be busy and constantly checking their phones for texts, email, or social-media updates. Yet to build relationships, you must get to know people, and to get to know them, you have to listen to them:

- **Give the person your full attention.** Look at the person with whom you are having a conversation, and don't let your eyes wander. Don't keep checking your phone, and *definitely* don't text. Get rid of any external distractions if you can. Close the door. Turn off any music.
- **Stop talking.** You can't talk and listen at the same time, no matter what some people may claim. Let the other person speak, and don't interrupt. And don't finish the other person's sentences, either.
- **Use verbal prompts.** These are brief comments that let the person know you are paying attention. Don't overdo it, but an occasional "Oh" or "I see" or "Okay" can be effective. This is crucial when you are on the phone. If you don't use verbal prompts, the person talking will often ask, "Are you there?" In person, you also can nod your head occasionally to indicate that you are listening.
- **Get the facts straight.** Ask the person questions to clarify the information he or she is imparting or to get additional information.
- **Check in.** Paraphrase the gist of the conversation. Saying "Let me make sure I am grasping what you are saying; you are suggesting . . ." allows you to make sure that what you heard is what the person intended.

13. Help! I'm in a Conversation and I Can't Get Out!

I tried to get out of a conversation by excusing myself and saying that I was going to the restroom. It didn't work. She followed me into the ladies' room!

Getting out of a conversation can be the hardest part, as that funny-but-true anecdote from a bookstore manager attests. Numerous people in my seminars tell me this. Some people will not get into a conversation because they don't know how to get out of a conversation. But it is possible to disengage, and it helps to remember these two things:

1. You need to have an exit line ready that clearly signals the end of the conversation, such as "Nice to meet you" or "Nice talking to you" or "See you next week at the meeting."

    Other possible exit lines include saying that you are going to the men's room or ladies' room (though this one doesn't always work!) or you are going to get food. Or you can say something like "Excuse me. I need to find my boss before he leaves."

2. Before you give the exit line, you *must* be the one talking. You make a *wrap comment*—that is, you comment about what the person said—and then you transition to your exit line. Remember to leave when *you* are talking. At that point, you are in control, and it is a much smoother exit.

TRY THIS SUGGESTION

If people are in your office and you cannot get them to leave, you stand up and say something like "This has been really informative" or "I look forward to following up with you at the next meeting." Usually, the visitors will get the hint.

14. Dodging Too-Personal Conversations

I just don't want to discuss my personal life at work.

It's often difficult to know how to respond when a customer, colleague, or any other acquaintance shows an interest in, or asks questions about, areas of your life that you consider personal.

In one of my business etiquette seminars, a young man made the statement above, and he asked how he should have responded to his manager when he inquired about his breakup with his fiancée. The young man felt very awkward discussing with his boss the details of his relationship with his fiancée.

The young man's communication concern often arises for all of us. How do we avoid talking about something that we don't want to discuss?

The first thing to remember is that you don't have to answer every question asked of you. I am not telling you to be rude. Rather, I am suggesting that you politely extricate yourself from the discussion. (Keep in mind that you do need to share a little about your life. If you don't, it's hard to make conversation with others. Plus, in the absence of any information, what your colleagues may imagine could be way worse than anything in your real life!)

Here are some options that will work for deflecting personal questions as well as any uncomfortable discussions:

- **Change the subject.** Ignore the question and start talking about something else. You could say something like "That reminds me; I wanted to talk to you about . . ."

- **Simply state the facts.** In the above situation, the young man had brought his fiancée to company functions, so people naturally asked about her. He needed to say something. He could answer the question directly but avoid all the details and not get into the drama of it. For example, "I am no longer engaged to Anna. I'm okay. I believe things work out for the best."

- **Leave the group.** If an awkward topic comes up in a group situation, give some reason for leaving and then leave. For example, "Oh, I just remembered that I have a phone call coming in to my office in a few minutes. I'll catch up with you later."

- **Be polite and powerful.** You could say, assertively, "I am uncomfortable discussing this, but thank you for your concern."

POINT TO PONDER

There are people who divulge too much. On a plane, a vice president found herself sitting in front of two employees of an advertising agency that her company used. The agency employees didn't know she was there. Without considering who might overhear, the two spoke about her company's business, as well as the business of other companies they represented, throughout the two-hour flight. The vice president heard all of it. Not surprisingly, she fired the agency.

15. Political Discussions to Avoid at Work

I couldn't believe that he wasn't voting for my candidate. I thought we were similar.

The client quoted above found herself on the opposite side of the political fence from the owner of a business with which she often dealt, and it affected her attitude toward him.

Anytime there's a big election looming—whether it's a nationwide presidential contest or a controversial local race—it can be tempting to get into political discussions at work. After all, you may figure, what's the harm in admitting who you think should win the election, or in giving your opinion about what should happen in Afghanistan?

The problem is that people often have strong opinions when it comes to politics. In today's supercharged political climate, it's easy to say something that might insult or enrage your boss, a customer, or a coworker. Political discussions can quickly and easily escalate into arguments, sometimes heated ones.

Yet it's frequently hard to avoid such discussions, particularly during major elections, as we are bombarded with political ads day and night. However, consider the consequences of discussing questions like the following, which should persuade you not to ask them or answer them:

1. **"Whom are you going to vote for?"** Never ask this question. You may get an answer you did not expect or want. Your opinion of that person may be altered permanently—and often negatively, if he or she is not voting for your candidate.

2. **"Who do you think won the debate?"** If a public or televised debate between candidates triggers a discussion in the office, you and your

colleague may have very different opinions about who answered questions effectively or who looked good behind the podium. Arguing these points usually will not resolve anything. If a colleague keeps pushing his or her opinion, you can say "Let's agree to disagree" and then change the subject.

3. **"How can you possibly vote for _____?"** Asking this question is not just commenting on the person's choice. It is putting the person down. Discussions can quickly become ugly after that.

4. **"Don't you think the candidate's stance on _____ is outrageous?"** Using strong negative language to discuss an issue can come across as "fighting words" to others. If you want to comment on an issue, a better way to word your disagreement would be, "I disagree with the candidate's position on _____ because of _____."

The negative impact of being drawn into political discussions by answering questions like the ones above is obvious. If you need a refresher on how to avoid the pitfalls, consult the suggestions in Etiquette 14, "Dodging Too-Personal Conversations."

POINT TO PONDER

Watch what you say in professional situations. An unguarded tongue can get you into trouble, even when the topic isn't politics.

A sales director at one of my global etiquette classes told me of an embarrassing situation he experienced, and we can all learn from his story.

The man and his wife were attending a cocktail reception in New York City. Since both were originally from Portugal, they used their native language to exchange some unflattering comments about the clothing worn by a woman who was standing near them. A few minutes later, the woman walked up to them and asked them a question—in perfect Portuguese. They were mortified.

I have heard similar stories over the years. Remember that wherever you are in the world, even when you least expect it, someone may understand the language you are speaking.

16. Thank You . . . No, Thank You

Mom, you taught me to say "Thank you" when I was a young child. Why do you have to teach this to adults?

My son asked me that question after listening to one of my speeches. It was an interesting question, since I assume most parents teach their children to say "Thank you" in appropriate situations. Unfortunately, in a world where everyone is always in a rush, it's easy to forget this little nicety.

When you convey thanks, you are acknowledging the kindness, thoughtfulness, or helpfulness shown to you by another person. There is no downside to this courtesy, and it is usually much appreciated by the recipient.

Monitor yourself, and make sure you are expressing thanks in the following situations:

1. **Say "Thank you" if someone helps you or goes above and beyond for you.** There can be negative consequences if you don't. One woman said that she gave a reference for a colleague looking for work. The man got the job, but he never thanked her. She said she would never help him again.

2. **Use "Thanks" as a closing in your emails**. Writing "Thanks" or "Thank you" is a quick and effective way to acknowledge someone's effort. When texting, you can use the shortcut "thx," if appropriate.

3. **Wave "Thanks" to the driver of a car that lets you into a line of traffic.** My husband says that men wave; women, all too frequently, don't. I hate to admit it, but he may be right. One colleague said she doesn't wave to men because she doesn't want the action viewed

as flirtatious. Although that can sometimes be a valid concern, most drivers see the wave as an acknowledgment of their kindness. Kindness begets kindness. One driver lets you into the line; you let someone else in; that person may extend the courtesy to a third driver. As a result, we all end up with an easier commute to work. And the person you wave to as you are driving to an interview just may be the person who will be interviewing you. Stranger things have happened.

4. **"Please" counts too.** In addition to expressing thanks, remember to say "Please" as well in appropriate situations. One administrative assistant said that she worked for five bosses. The boss who added "Please" to his requests was the boss who got his work done first.

POINT TO PONDER

"On the way to work," a store manager told me, "I gave a rude gesture to a driver when he cut me off. I can't believe the next day the driver just happened to walk into my store, and when he saw me, he said, 'You're the one that gave me the finger.' He was not happy."

My son knew at an early age the importance of expressing thanks, including saying "No, thank you." One night when he was a toddler, I said to Jacob, "It's time for bed." He smiled and responded, "Oh, no, thank you, Mommy."

Q. *I have a tendency to say "Thank you" a lot. Is it possible to say "Thank you" too often?*

A. You need to say it only once or twice within a conversation. Otherwise, you may dilute its impact and possibly make yourself seem somewhat helpless and needy.

17. Thank You Notes Do Matter

I am writting to thank you and to see how your shoe were.

I visited a specialty store to purchase a pair of shoes. My salesperson was very friendly and competent. However, my opinion of his professionalism changed when he sent me the above thank you note—unsigned and containing careless errors.

It's not enough to be mindful of saying thanks for kindnesses extended to you. You should also write thank you notes when circumstances warrant it. But be careful what you write.

Poorly written thank you notes with spelling and grammatical errors can be costly to your professional image and career advancement.

Consider the young man who had applied to be included in a management training program within his company. He did very well during his interviews, but afterward he sent a thank you note containing typos. He wasn't selected for the program—his potential bosses weren't confident that he would pay attention to details.

A well-written note can help you stand out from the competition, but one that is poorly done may damage your reputation. Professionals in human resources often use thank you notes as one of the ways in which they evaluate potential candidates.

Make sure you follow these guidelines so your notes project the right message:

- **Send thank you notes after significant occasions.** You should send a note after visiting someone's home, being treated to a meal, receiving a present, or interviewing for a job. You can also send thank you notes when people provide extra help for you or when you want to praise an employee or vendor.

Recently, a young woman I met for coffee wrote, "I am so thankful for all the time you spent with me and the help you have given me to begin my future." I would certainly help her again.

- **Don't make mistakes.** A typo, a misused word, or a confusing sentence can undermine your credibility. Before writing your actual note, create a draft of what you want to say, then carefully reread it—or have a trusted colleague do so—to make sure you haven't included errors.

- **Choose email or a handwritten note.** Writing an email note is the quick, informal way to say thanks; a handwritten note is the more personal way. For handwritten notes, the type of paper is important. Good quality, five-by-seven-inch paper or a folded note card are both appropriate. Have your name printed on the stationery, but don't make it very official looking.

  Before you choose between email and handwritten notes, consider that regular mail may take several days to get to its destination, while email arrives almost immediately. This time difference can be important after a job interview, if the hiring decision is being made quickly. Consider the following scenario:

  A human resources director interviewed four people for a job on a Tuesday. On Wednesday, she received email thank you notes from three of the four candidates. On Friday, she made her decision, but she did not consider the candidate from whom she had not received a note. On Monday, she received a handwritten note from the fourth candidate—which, of course, was too late.

- **Send notes within 24 hours.** Don't be like the woman who wrote, "I couldn't let another month go by without thanking you." But a late thank you note is better than no note. Send separate notes to all who need to be thanked.

Q. *I had recommended a colleague for a new position, and when the colleague got the job, she sent a thank you note and a small gift. Do I need to send a thank you note for the thank you gift?*

A. Technically you don't need to write a thank you note for a thank you gift, especially if the gift is given in person. But in this case, you may want to send an email congratulating the colleague on her new position and acknowledging the gift.

18. Refined Regifting Rules . . . Really!

I was really pleased that my coworker gave me a lovely photo book—until I found a card that indicated the gift had originally been given to her.

Ouch. Clearly that was a negligent gift giver. But is it generally okay to regift in a business environment?

In today's economy, regifting can be sound fiscal policy. Why let a perfectly good plant or fruitcake go to waste? Yet, how you regift is important. You always want the receiver of the gift to feel valued.

Here are seven guidelines for refined regifting:

1. **Make sure the gift is appropriate.** Don't just regift to get rid of an item. Give a gift that the recipient will like, use, and enjoy.

2. **Don't leave evidence of past gifting on the gift.** You don't want to damage your relationship with the person to whom you are giving the gift. Check the item carefully and remove any indication that you were given the gift previously.

3. **Don't give the same gift back to the giver.** "Oh, that looks familiar!" is not what you want to hear when a person opens your gift. Keep a list of the gifts you receive and who gave them to you, as well as a list of the gifts you give and to whom.

4. **Make sure the gift is in good condition.** Check the item carefully, and make sure the sell-by dates on food items have not expired. You may need to rewrap the gift, but don't use boxes that indicate the gift came from a specific store when it didn't.

5. **Be careful regifting items that the recipient may want to exchange, unless you have the gift receipt.** The recipient of the gift may ask

you where you purchased the item in order to exchange it for a different size or color.

6. **Tell the person it's a regift if the gift is really special for that person.** A colleague who was given tickets to a concert regifted them to her best customer because she knew the featured band was his favorite. She told him that she knew he would enjoy the show more than she would. The customer was thrilled.

7. **Be polite.** If you receive a gift that you know is a regift, you must still say "Thank you." And if the item isn't for you, follow the above regifting guidelines.

Q. *Is it okay to give my boss a gift? I keep hearing it's not.*

A. You generally don't give the boss a gift. It can look like you are trying to curry favor. Yet in small offices, many times the boss and an employee will become friendly and exchange gifts at the holidays or on birthdays.

POINT TO PONDER

Many companies have restrictions on what gifts, if any, employees may accept from vendors or customers. Make sure you are familiar with these restrictions, and follow them.

---

19. Love Me . . . Love Me Not!
Office Romance Restrictions

Given the amount of time Americans spend at work, it's probably inevitable that some office relationships will develop into office romances.

But romance at work can be costly. Even CEOs aren't immune to the fallout from romantic entanglements at work. Consider a handful of headline-making resignations in recent years:

- Stryker Chief Executive Stephen P. MacMillan resigned in early 2012 following questions about his relationship with a former flight attendant for the company's corporate jets.

- Best Buy's former chief executive Brian Dunn resigned in 2012 after allegations that a personal relationship with a 29-year-old subordinate "negatively impacted the work environment."

- Mark Hurd resigned in 2010 as CEO of Hewlett-Packard after an internal investigation into his relationship with a contractor.

Workers lower on the corporate ladder might not have such high-profile case resolutions, but even single, consenting adults need to be careful about how they conduct personal relationships with colleagues.

Before becoming involved with a coworker, make sure you know your company's policies on dating because you don't want to violate any corporate regulations. If you don't behave properly, an office romance can cause conflict and have a negative impact on your career.

Here are some guidelines to help you and your significant other share a copier by day and a bedroom by night without hurting your professional image:

- **Do not broadcast your relationship on any social-media sites.** Keep the relationship private. Your coworkers do not need to know the intimate details of your romance. No posting information or photos about your latest love interest on Facebook or sending tweets about it. You never know who will see them.

- **Don't vent negative feelings.** Another downside to workplace relationships occurs when a love affair dissolves: you may still have to see or work with the person. You can't vent your negative feelings in public, even if the person treated you poorly. If the relationship fails, be professional and adult about it.

- **Don't engage in physical contact in the office.** No romantic displays. No kissing, hugging, or hand-holding in the office. This also includes your behavior at office parties.

- **Your boss shouldn't be your Valentine.** Relationships are difficult enough without having your boss or a subordinate as your Valentine. If you are dating your boss, arrange to report to someone else; and if you are the boss, arrange to have your subordinate report to somebody else before you start dating.

20. Starbucks Is My Office!
Working Remotely

The man looked like he had moved into the coffee shop. He was using two tables, had files all over, and he had six dirty coffee cups around him. But maybe that was his plan. Like everybody else, I sat as far away from him as I could.

Many workers today are working remotely. According to some reports, as many as 37 million people telecommute full- or part-time. By encouraging telecommuting, companies reduce their need for office space and often gain productivity from their workers, and workers gain flexibility and eliminate their commuting time.

Whether your home office is really at your home or at a Wi-Fi–equipped coffee shop such as Starbucks, you need to be professional when interacting with potential customers, clients, vendors, colleagues, and bosses. Don't be like the gentleman described above, whom I encountered when meeting a colleague for coffee. Here are guidelines to help you maintain a business image no matter where your office is located:

1. **Have a separate space for your office.** If you are working from home, you need an area or room that is private and removed from the distractions of your personal life. Having a dedicated "place" will allow you to focus on your work. Think about how your home schedule may interfere with your work, and adjust accordingly. Reschedule any work being done so the noise doesn't interfere with any scheduled calls. "I couldn't believe it; he arranged the call and I could barely hear him," one business owner told me about a vendor who was seeking her business. "His landscaper started mowing the lawn just as we started our conversation."

If your office is your local coffee shop, you need to observe some common courtesies. Don't hog tables. Do order more than a cup of coffee, clean up after yourself, be polite to the other customers, be nice to the staff, and tip generously.

2. **Answer your phone or cell phone professionally.** Invest in a separate line for calls. When you answer, give a greeting and your name: "Good morning, Barbara Pachter speaking." When you are not able to answer the phone, have your callers hear a businesslike message—no little kids talking or music blasting. And don't discuss private matters in public spaces nor have your conversation affect the other people in the shop.

3. **Keep in touch with other employees.** Use the phone, email, texting, instant messaging, Skype, and the like to maintain connections. Don't broadcast that you're at the ball game. You may have started working at 5 a.m. so you could take time out in the afternoon, but coworkers usually don't want to hear about it!

4. **Take off those PJs.** "On the fourth day of telecommuting, I realized that clothes are totally unnecessary," said Scott Adams, creator of the comic strip *Dilbert*. Cute, but not necessarily an example to emulate—especially if you are communicating with the office via Skype. There are lots of testimonials from telecommuters about the joys of working in pajamas, but it's a good idea to dress somewhat professionally. Studies have shown that how we dress influences how we behave, and that holds true whether we are at the corporate HQ or behind closed doors at home.

5. **Have face-to-face interactions when you can**. One young man complained about a telecommuter on his team: "She lives close to the office and has no problem asking me to do things for her, yet I have never seen her face." You don't want to seem out of reach or be forgotten. So meet people for coffee or lunch. If you don't have a regular day in the office, attend the occasional meeting, or if you live too far away for that, make sure you attend company retreats or conferences.

Q. *I am new to the workplace and have a long commute. I think I want to telecommute. How do I approach my boss?*

A. Before you approach your boss about telecommuting, create a well-thought-out plan about how you could successfully accomplish your work from home. But remember there is a lot to learn by being in an office, especially since you are just starting your career. You can meet more people, learn about other jobs within the company, and gain knowledge about your company and workplace.

An alternative to telecommuting may be to change your working hours so the commute is less stressful. You also could turn the long commute into a positive: listen to audio books if you're driving, or read a book or study for a course if you're using public transportation.

21. Allow Me . . . No, Allow Me: "Helping Etiquette" Guidelines

When I'm at work, I don't expect a man to help me on with my coat, yet when I go out with my husband, I hand him my coat so he can help me. Is that crazy?

This question from a seminar participant brings up the area of *helping etiquette*—those gender niceties that include men helping women with their coats, carrying their packages, or opening their doors. Both men and women can struggle with knowing the appropriate behaviors because what they do in their personal life may be different from what is acceptable in their business environment.

In the social world many men help women, as illustrated by the above question. Yet many of the ways in which men and women interact have changed in today's business world, as gender has been put aside in favor of professional standing, or whether one is the host or the visitor.

Shouldn't you be able to help someone? Of course you should, and you can. Both men and women should help each other if the other person wants help.

Yet, if the assistance is overdone, the woman can be viewed as someone who needs to be taken care of (or supported). This is not an image a woman wants to project if she wants more responsibility and influence in an organization.

Here are six areas that can be confusing for both men and women in business and some strategies for dealing with them:

1. **Carrying packages.** Offer to carry packages for anyone who needs help, regardless of gender.

2. **Putting on coats.** The rule is the same as the one above: help anyone who needs it, whether male or female.

3. **Opening the door.** Whoever gets to the door first, regardless of gender, should open it and hold it for the person behind him or her. Also, it is a very gracious host who subtly gets to the door first and opens it and holds it for the guest. And it is a very smart junior person who unobtrusively gets to the door first and opens it and holds it for the more senior person.

POINT TO PONDER

Make sure you say "Thanks!" if someone holds the door for you. It's rude not to acknowledge this considerate act.

What if someone doesn't thank you? People have told me that when someone doesn't express thanks, they will sarcastically say, "You're welcome." I don't recommend this response, at work or anywhere else.

---

4. **Pulling out the chair.** Both men and women can pull out their own chairs.

5. **Ordering the food.** The guest should order first, regardless of gender. If the host is a woman and the waiter comes to her first, she can say, "Oh, please take my guest's order first."

6. **Paying the bill.** If you did the inviting, you are the host, and you should pay the bill, regardless of gender. What if a male guest wants to pay? A woman does have some choices. She can say, "Oh, it's not me; it is the firm that is paying." Or she can excuse herself from the table and pay the bill away from the guests. This option works for men as well, and it is a very refined way to pay a bill. However, the bottom line is that you don't want to fight over a bill. If a male guest insists on paying despite a female host's best efforts, let him pay.

PART 2

MAINTAINING A PROFESSIONAL IMAGE

> You must realize that if you aren't managing your own professional image, someone else is.
>
> —Professor Laura Morgan Roberts,
> Harvard Business School

What do others see when you walk into a room?

You always project an image—when you attend a meeting, when you make a presentation, even when you meet a colleague in the hallway. You have no control over how others see you. None. But you can control what you are sending out.

I believe that if you project a confident, credible, composed image, people will respond to you as if you *are* all those things. Who cares what you are feeling on the inside! For most of us, the inside eventually will catch up with the outside.

To a large extent, your professional image is based on your verbal and nonverbal communications and your ability to establish rapport. We have already discussed rapport building, so let's consider verbal and nonverbal communications skills.

The *verbal* is made up of the actual words you use.

The *nonverbal* includes the following:

- **Your body language:** Posture, eye contact, gestures, and facial expression

- **Your dress:** The clothes you wear, their fit, their style, and appropriateness

- **Your voice:** Your vocal volume and how quickly you speak

As a senior vice president I once coached at a consulting firm told me, "I attribute a lot of my success to your instruction. I still shudder to think of the oversized dress shirts and too-big pants I used to wear." He recognizes that his professional image in combination with his business skills have helped him seal many a deal.

22. Body Language:
What Your Posture Projects

The woman walked into the room with her shoulders hunched forward, her back rounded, and her eyes downcast. Nobody knew she was the new vice president until she went to the podium to speak to her employees, but by then she had lost all leadership credibility with her audience.

Flo, a fictional insurance company spokesperson on television and radio, said during one radio advertisement, "I'm sure you're a great person with great posture." (Progressive Insurance)

A participant in one of my seminars said that as soon as she saw me walk into the room, she knew I was the instructor.

All of the illustrations above hint at the importance of posture—of standing erect and projecting confidence.

What does your posture say about you?

To stand confidently, keep your legs aligned with your shoulders, feet about four to six inches apart. Your weight should be distributed equally on both legs. Don't cross your legs or tilt your head. Your chin should be up—not way up, but up. Your body should not be rigid. Shoulders should be back—not way back, but not forward either. And unless you are gesturing, your hands can be down at your sides.

This is an assertive posture. It is a posture that projects confidence, not insecurity. You are open to the person to whom you are talking. And you can stand tall, regardless of your height.

Don't assume you have good posture until you get feedback confirming that you do. Start taking note of other people's posture—you will be amazed at how many people stand passively.

Women especially have a tendency to stand with their legs crossed and hands folded in front, or with their weight pressed down on one hip. Either way, the position is not grounded, and it comes across as very submissive. They are taking up as little space as possible. Men also can stand passively. They put their feet together, or they sway back and forth as they play with the keys in their pockets.

If enhancing your career isn't sufficient reason to make you stand tall, maybe the threat of pain will do it. An advertisement for an over-the-counter pain medication warns: "Don't slouch. Poor posture can cause a headache."

TRY THIS SUGGESTION

Increase your awareness of the way you stand. Check your posture at different times during the day, and observe other people. Have someone record you on video, and take note of what needs correcting in your posture. You can't change what you don't know you are doing. (Video feedback is useful for discovering and correcting a variety of nonverbal behaviors.)

23. If Crossing Your Legs
Turns Women into Ladies,
What Does It Do to Matt Lauer?

During an etiquette seminar, a participant asked what I thought about the fact that Elena Kagan, then a Supreme Court nominee, "did not cross her legs like a lady" when she met with power brokers on Capitol Hill.

Her question was prompted by a mini-controversy stirred up by Robin Givhan, the fashion critic formerly at the *Washington Post*, when she wrote about Kagan's sitting position during her meeting with Senator Amy Klobuchar. In the photograph that appeared with the story, Kagan had both feet firmly planted on the floor; Klobuchar had her legs crossed. Other journalists weighed in on Givhan's story, and several headlines stated, "Why Kagan Won't Cross Her Legs Like a Lady?"

My first thought was, "Why are journalists discussing the sitting posture of a Supreme Court nominee?"

In her article, Givhan indicated that although a lot of women sit with their legs crossed, Kagan could not be bullied into conformity. As a former news photographer, I know that sometimes a photograph is just a photograph! Other pictures from that meeting may have shown Kagan sitting in other positions.

Yes, a lot of women do sit with their legs crossed. But consider these points:

- **It's not for women only.** Both men and women sit with their legs crossed. When teen idol Justin Bieber did an impression of Matt Lauer on the *TODAY Show*, for instance, he crossed his legs as Lauer often does during interviews. So much for being a lady!

- **Crossing your legs can be distracting.** If a woman wears a short skirt and crosses her legs, she projects a very sexy, too-thigh-revealing image.

The bottom line, however, is health related: crossing your legs is bad for your circulation because it increases the pressure on your veins. We shouldn't do it, and we shouldn't judge anyone—including a Supreme Court justice—on whether she does or doesn't cross her legs.

24. Your Hands Are Talking, but What Are They Saying?

One of my corporate assignments was to observe a presentation by a CEO of a major company and to give him feedback. During our conversation, I asked him, "Why were you nervous?" He was uncomfortable with the question and demanded, "How did you know I was nervous?" I responded, "You played with a rubber band the whole time you were speaking, and your audience noticed."

An important part of mastering body language is knowing what your hands are saying.

You may be unaware of your hands when you give a speech or engage in conversation, but they are conveying information nonetheless. Make sure the message they are sending is the one you intend.

Whether you are interviewing for a job, meeting with a colleague, or negotiating with a vendor, keep in mind these pointers:

- **Keep your hands close to your body.** If they invade somebody else's personal space, it can be perceived as aggressiveness.

- **Resist the urge to twist your hair or jiggle coins in your pocket.** You will drive others crazy if you indulge in these activities. Also pen-clickers, hand-wringers, and rubber-band stretchers all reveal nervousness. Remember, it is okay to be nervous, but do not show it.

TRY THIS SUGGESTION

Don't hold any items in your hands when you are speaking. It's too easy to play with something if you are holding it.

- **Point with an open palm, and keep your fingers together**. If you point with your index finger, it appears aggressive. Both men and women point, but women have a tendency to do it more than men. Women often find out that they are pointing when their children do it back to them. (Those preschoolers learned it from someone!) There is another aggressive gesture—pounding on the table—that both men and women engage in at times, but men have a tendency to do this more. It can be very intimidating to others, even if your intention is simply to emphasize a point. The words you are speaking may be okay, but the pounding makes your statement aggressive.

- **Clasped hands, or one hand placed over the other, can indicate humility and deference.** Do you want to convey this message?

- **Keep your body "open" by resisting the urge to cross your arms.** Crossed arms can make you appear defensive or "closed." (This point involves more than your hands, but it's an important gesture to understand.)

- **Don't place your hands on your hips**. This can seem either aggressive or arrogant.

- **Don't inspect your fingernails or tap your fingers on the desk while someone else is talking**. It looks like you are bored, and it's distracting.

25. Face-Off: Don't Discount Your Facial Expression

Do you know your *standard facial expression*?

This is my term for what people see when you are looking at them, listening to them, or just not talking. Many people have very stern facial expressions, and they don't realize it.

One example of this was the engineer for a radio station where I was talking about standard facial expression. After the show, the engineer came up to me and said, "You know, lady, you may have something with this standard facial expression. My girlfriend keeps asking me if I am mad at her. I'm not. Maybe it's my face." And it *was* his face—or more precisely, his expression!

There can be career consequences to having a severe standard facial expression. People may avoid you, think you are mad at them, or get defensive around you. These are not good outcomes if you want to connect with people.

What is your standard facial expression saying about you? One woman said she learned how severe her standard facial expression was when she saw her wedding video. She said, "It was the happiest day of my life, and I looked miserable."

TRY THIS SUGGESTION

Pay attention to the unsolicited comments you receive from friends and colleagues. Do people often ask you if you are upset? It could be your face.

You want to seem approachable. You can learn to control your facial muscles so that your normal expression conveys "pleasant" rather than "peeved." You've probably heard the expression "smiling with your eyes"— try it! You might be surprised at how many more people smile back at you.

Remember too that the eyes are a key part of our interactions with others. In this culture, it is important to look at someone when you are speaking to him or her. We don't really trust people if we can't see their eyes.

A police training officer asked me if I could help his officers to understand that they needed to take off their dark glasses when they were talking to people. With their eyes hidden behind dark glasses, they came across as very intimidating.

Many of us have a tendency to look away in an uncomfortable situation. By doing this, you are telling the other person that you are nervous. You don't want to do that. Force yourself to look at the person—though you can occasionally glance away.

POINT TO PONDER

Eye contact plays a big role in hiring decisions. In a CareerBuilder survey of more than 2,500 hiring managers, more than 67 percent said they would be less likely to hire someone who failed to make eye contact, 38 percent were reluctant to give a job to someone who didn't smile, and 33 percent had a similar reaction to applicants who fidgeted too much.

26. Speak Up! We Can't Hear You

As a young woman was leaving the office, her boss started giving her assignments. She replied, "But I'm in training this afternoon." He ignored her comments and continued to describe the tasks in more detail. It dawned on the young woman—who had recently attended my seminar on this topic—that he hadn't heard her. She raised her volume and repeated, "I'm in training this afternoon." He replied, "Oh, sure. You can do it tomorrow. Have a good class!"

Many men and women, especially women, do not speak loudly enough. And speaking softly is a subtle nonverbal action that can affect your professionalism.

Have you ever said something in a meeting and nobody responded? Then, 20 minutes later, somebody at the end of the table said exactly what you said—and that person was acknowledged for it.

It could be that by speaking softly, you make it easy for people to ignore your comments. You are not being heard with what I call *substance*. This is the quality that ensures that what you say registers on others.

POINT TO PONDER

A woman recently emailed me for help. She admitted that she spoke so softly that people had started to refer to her as "Wendy Whispers."

Not speaking loudly enough can invite errors too. One soft-spoken supervisor was giving instructions involving numbers to two employees. One employee heard 3; the other heard 30. Big difference!

You usually can add power to your presence by adding volume. But you don't want to shout either. Follow these three suggestions so your professionalism is not hurt by your volume:

1. **Monitor yourself.** If you find yourself thinking "But I told him that the first time," it's possible that you are not speaking with enough volume.

2. **Gain an awareness of your volume.** Listen to your voice mail messages before you send them. If necessary, redo the message and increase your volume.

3. **Learn your range.** People who are soft-spoken usually believe that they have a choice only between their regular soft volume and screaming. Everybody has a range of volume—you need to learn yours. Count slowly from 1 to 5, increasing your volume with each number. Number 1 is your softest volume, and 5 is screaming. Most people should aim to keep their volume between 2½ and 3½.

POINT TO PONDER

Prime Minister Margaret Thatcher, subject of the 2012 film *The Iron Lady*, took elocution lessons to lower her "too feminine" voice.

27. The Do-Not-Say List

After discussing self-discounting language in a communications class, a participant suggested that I create a "do-not-say list." I thought it was a great idea. Having a list of phrases to avoid can help people steer clear of language that could have a negative impact on their careers, particularly if used frequently.

Listed below are my top six suggestions for the Do-Not-Say List. Using these comments in business (and life) can diminish your stature in the eyes of others, minimize what you are saying, or tarnish your professional image:

1. **"Can I ask a question?"** You don't have to ask permission; just ask the question.

2. **"I'm sorry to bother you."** Why are you a bother? You can say, "Excuse me. Do you have a moment?"

3. **"I was hoping that you could spare a few moments."** Same as above. Simply say, "Excuse me. Do you have a moment?"

4. **"Thank you for listening to me."** At the end of a presentation, you should say, "Thank you." This lets the audience know that the presentation is over. You don't have to thank people for listening to you. Aren't your comments and opinions worthwhile?

5. **"I will be honest with you."** Aren't you *always* honest? You don't need to use this phrase.

6. **"I was just wondering if perhaps . . ."** This phrase is a passive way of asking a question or backing into a statement. You can eliminate "I was just wondering if perhaps" and simply ask a question or

make a statement. Instead of "I was just wondering if perhaps there will be enough computers for the project?" you can say, "Will there be enough computers for the project?"

28. Why I Think You Should Avoid "I Think"

How would you answer your boss if she asked, "What time is the luncheon on Friday?" Would you say "The luncheon is at noon" or "I think the luncheon is at noon"?

If you picked the first sentence as your response, you are indicating that you know the information and have answered with certainty. But if you chose the second sentence, you appear unsure about your answer. By saying "I think," you are telling your boss that you really don't know.

Why would you tell someone that you don't know something when you do?

A woman in one of my seminars told me that she had just done this. Even though she knew that the time for a meeting had changed, when her boss asked about it, she prefaced her answer with "I think." After hearing her response, the boss immediately walked over to the phone and called someone else to get the information.

Using "I think" can also make you appear wishy-washy. My son asked to go somewhere, and I responded, "I think it will be okay." He responded, "Mom, do you think so, or do you know so?" (He has been a seminar participant all his life!)

People tell me that they use "I think" because they don't want to come on too strong or appear too opinionated, especially with a higher-level person.

I respond to these comments with, "I think there are alternatives. . . ." No, of course I don't say that! I respond without the "I think" and say, "There are alternatives that will allow you to appear confident without being too authoritative." These include the following:

- **Eliminate the "I think" and just state the information.** Instead of "I think another thing I want to say is . . . ,"simply say, "Another thing I want to say is . . ." Make sure there is no harsh tone to your voice.

- **Use "I suggest" or "I recommend" when asked to give your opinion about which product, service, or person to choose.** Instead of "I think Product X," say, "I suggest Product X" or "After my research, I recommend Product X." You could, in some circumstances, keep it neutral and say, "Product X meets our requirements."

WATCH YOUR USE OF FILLER WORDS

A woman I coached said "Right, right, right, right" constantly when she agreed with what was being said. She had no idea she was doing this until I pointed it out to her. Once she realized, she wondered whether she had been driving people crazy with her unconscious habit.

All of us occasionally use *filler words* such as *um*, *all right*, or *okay*. But if your use of such words becomes a pattern, people will notice, and it will detract from your image. People may even start counting how often you use a specific filler word—and that means they won't be listening to what you have to say.

We do not expect people to be perfect, but we do expect them to be professional. Find out if you are using too many filler words by listening to your voice mail messages before you send them. Or ask a trusted friend to point out every time you use a filler word.

Once you have identified your filler words, you usually can catch them right after you have said them, and eventually you will be able to stop saying them altogether.

29. Is Your Diction Affecting Your Professional Image?

A participant in a recent communications seminar told me about her experience in another training session, where the instructor used the phrase "All's you gotta do." After she heard that phrase, she stopped listening.

In the above example, the instructor's use of nonstandard language detracted from his message. It may not be fair, but people often judge others on the quality of their diction. They may make negative assumptions about someone's intelligence or education based on that person's word choice.

We may pick up the use of these nonstandard words from their use in marketing or creative fields.

Among the phrases I have heard used in business are the following:

- **"Are youse finished with the project?"** Use just *you*. The word *you* is both singular and plural in the English language.

- **"Didya get to the meeting on time?"** Use *did you*.

- **"All's you gotta do."** According to an article in the *New York Times*,* *all's* started off as a contraction of *all as*, but it is generally considered a substandard word today. Instead of *all's*, use *all*, and instead of *gotta*, use *have to*.

- **"I'm gonna get it for you."** Use *I'm going to* or *I am going to*.

---

* http://www.nytimes.com/2010/09/12/magazine/12onlanguage.html.

Monitor the way you speak. Do you use any of the above expressions? Years ago, I discovered that I was saying *gonna*, but I didn't realize it until a speech coach pointed it out to me.

POINT TO PONDER

Be careful if you evaluate your diction using the speech-to-text button on your phone, as it will often correct your comments and therefore not alert you to sloppy speech patterns. Using the button, I consciously said "Didya," and the text appeared as "Did you."

30. I'm Sorry, I Can't Apologize

A colleague missed an appointment with a vendor. She called the vendor to apologize. Thinking about the conversation later, she realized that she had said "I'm sorry" numerous times. She called me and asked if you can say "I'm sorry" too much.

Surprisingly, I said "Yes." Since I teach etiquette, I would never tell anyone to be rude. If you trip someone, spill coffee (or anything else) on somebody, or inadvertently hurt someone's feelings, it is appropriate to say "I'm sorry." And if you work in customer service, saying you are sorry may be part of your job description. However, my friend brought up one of several areas where people (often women, but men as well) overuse "I'm sorry" and, as a result, detract from their professional image.

Consider the following behaviors, and ask yourself if you practice any of them:

1. **Repeat "I'm sorry" numerous times.** If you say "I'm sorry," say it only once. Are you any sorrier the sixth time than you were the first time? Of course not. A long time ago, I was a "serial apologizer." I would repeat "I'm sorry" so often that my friends joked that on my gravestone they would put, "I'm sorry, I can't apologize."

POINT TO PONDER

A colleague asked a woman during their conversation why she said "I'm sorry" so much. She replied, "I'm sorry?"

2. **Put yourself down.** Using such phrases as "I'm sorry to disturb you" or "I'm sorry to bother you" can draw into question your

67

self-esteem. Why are you a "bother"? (This expression is also on the Do-Not-Say List.) Your work is valuable also. Instead of apologizing, you can say, politely but assertively, "Excuse me. Do you have a minute?"

3. **Take responsibility for something that isn't your fault.** If you say "I'm sorry," you are implying that you are the one to blame. A man returned from lunch and said, "It's raining outside." His colleague responded, "I'm sorry," as if the rain were her responsibility. If she wanted to say something, she could have made a neutral comment such as, "I hear the rain will continue all day." In other situations, you can explain. Instead of "I'm sorry I missed the meeting," one manager said, "I had every intention of joining you, but my day took a different turn." She then explained that she had been involved in a minor car accident. (Note that this was not a fabricated excuse but the actual reason she had missed the meeting.)

4. **Say "I'm sorry" when it is your fault.** This occurs when you have done something that you shouldn't have done, such as inadvertently giving out wrong information. Many of my seminar participants struggle with this issue, and it can become a heated discussion. Some believe very strongly that saying "I'm sorry" is the polite thing to do. Others believe, just as strongly, that you need only acknowledge the mistake and that it is not necessary to apologize. Who's correct? There is no absolute answer.

One CEO told me that when his employees say "I'm sorry," he thinks they are asking him for forgiveness. He would much rather they admit the problem and tell him how they plan to fix it. Consider these two responses: "I'm so sorry I messed up" or "You are correct. There were mistakes made. It won't happen again." I believe the second choice is more powerful.

POINT TO PONDER

Don't confuse the excessive use of "I'm sorry" in a business context with expressions of sympathy. Saying "I'm sorry" to somebody who has suffered a loss is not only okay but it is also no doubt comforting to the person hearing it.

31. Do You Talk Too Much?
Let Me Count the Ways!

An executive asked me for suggestions to help an employee who talked too much and, as a result, limited her opportunities for advancement. The executive found the approach outlined below to be helpful because it attempts to identify the root of the problem before trying to correct it:

1. **Identify how the overtalking occurs.** You can't eliminate what you don't know you are doing. Here are four possibilities:

   - **Giving too much information:** During a meeting a supervisor was asked where he had bought his watch. Instead of saying, "At a great local store when I was on vacation in San Francisco," he went into a five-minute monologue about searching six stores to find the perfect watch. Just answer the question. If people need more detail, they will ask you.

   - **Using too many words:** Instead of "Let's get together next week," the person will say, "I was just thinking that, you know, if you have some time and are not busy, we ought to get together next week." Say what you need to say in as few words as necessary.

   - **Repeating what someone said in different words:** Some repetition can confirm to the other person that you have heard what he or she said. But in a group meeting, too much repetition can be viewed as one-upmanship—the need to let everyone know you also knew that information.

   - **Talking when you shouldn't:** This includes whispering to a co-worker during a presentation or not reading the cues from meeting participants that no more discussion is needed.

2. **Ask a trusted colleague or coach to help.** This person can point out when you are talking too much. Others are probably aware of your loquaciousness even if you aren't. One man who was about to be coached for promotion sought help from his marketing team on what problems he needed to address. Immediately, the newest member of the team remarked, "Well, you talk too much."

3. **Use your voice mail system.** As we have suggested elsewhere in this book, listen to how you describe something on the messages you leave for others. If you are too wordy, redo the message.

4. **Check in with yourself.** Before you add your comments during a meeting, ask yourself, "Do I really need to say this?"

TRY THIS SUGGESTION

Come up with a solution that works for you. Be creative. One manager puts the initials KIS at the top of his papers as a reminder to "keep it short" when he speaks at meetings.

32. Be Direct! You're More Likely to Get What You Want

A colleague of mine was walking with his six-year-old son, and before they crossed the street, he asked his boy, "Do you want to hold hands?" His son said, "No." His father replied, "Please hold my hand," and his son gave him his hand.

This story illustrates a little-known yet powerful communication approach that I teach in my seminars.

Using a *direct assertive statement* ("Please hold my hand") states what you want, and as result, you are more likely to get it. You have been clear and direct.

Using a *question* ("Do you want to hold hands?"), which is a softer way of expressing yourself, lets the other person make the choice, and you may not get what you want. You are being less direct.

After a two-hour meeting on a new proposal, one sales manager said to a colleague, "Would you like to go out to lunch to finalize the details?" By using a question, he gave the decision-making power to the other person, who could simply say "No." Had he said, "Let's finalize the details over lunch at XYZ," he would have been more likely to get the response he sought.

Pay attention to the way you word comments and requests. You may be falling into a pattern of just using questions and giving away your power as a result. Even with the boss, you can politely use a direct assertive statement. Consider the difference between "I'd like to go to the conference next week" and giving your reasons versus "Can I go to the conference next week?"

However, context is important. Sometimes, you may choose to use a question when talking up the ladder.

POINTS TO PONDER

It's not only at the office that direct, assertive statements pay off:

1. A few years ago, while walking on the boardwalk in Atlantic City, I said to my husband, "Hon, let's go to the casino tonight." He responded, "Okay." We walked a little more, and then, out of curiosity, I asked, "Hon, if I had asked you, 'Do you want to go to the casino tonight?' what would you have said?" He responded immediately. His answer would have been an unequivocal "No."

2. After learning about this communication technique, a woman started saying to her husband, "I need some money," and she got the cash. In the past she had asked, "Can I have some money?" and it started an argument.

33. What to Do
If You Are Interrupted

Do you catch yourself mouthing the words you think the other person in the conversation is going to say? Do you finish the speaker's words just to move the conversation along?

If you answered yes to either of these questions, you may be an interrupter.

People don't like to be interrupted. Nor do they like to be excluded from a conversation or to have their contributions ignored. While conducting research for my book *The Power of Positive Confrontation*, I discovered that interrupting is one of the 12 behaviors that most often cause conflict in the workplace.

Your credibility may be hurt if you respond rudely when someone interrupts you. Here are five options to try if you are interrupted—that is, if you are sure that you aren't a conversation hog:

1. **Let it go.** People occasionally interrupt one another.

2. **Continue speaking.** Many times the person trying to interrupt will stop talking. You may need to raise your volume a little to make sure the person hears you, but don't shout.

3. **Say something.** Try a polite but powerful response such as "I'll get to that in a moment," "Hold that thought," "Excuse me—I wasn't finished," or "I'm still talking." Deliver your line in a neutral, not harsh, tone of voice.

4. **Wait until the interrupter has finished speaking**. You can then say, "As I was saying . . ." Make sure this doesn't sound sarcastic.

5. **Confront the person privately.** If someone frequently interrupts you, talk to that person. Let him know that he has a tendency to inter-

rupt you, and you want it to stop. The interrupter may not be aware of his behavior.

Q. *What should I do? In my meetings, people interrupt each other a lot. I think my habit of waiting for others to finish what they are saying before I speak is seen as a weakness.*

A. In some situations, if you *don't* interrupt you won't get your voice heard. I'm not saying it's right, but it can be the reality in some meetings. To interrupt someone smoothly, wait until that person takes a breath—and everyone at some point does take a breath. You then jump in, acknowledge what the person was saying, and add your thoughts. You can say something like, "That's only part of the solution; if we look at . . ."

---

34. Are You Really Going to Wear That?

I am truly surprised at the amount of comment I have received in regards to my new attire, . . . including from my boss and the president of the company. It was my hope the change would not be as noticeable, but it appears it was more dramatic than I first believed.

—A general manager who reluctantly upgraded his wardrobe

Even in today's business casual environment, I get numerous questions from bosses, employees, and even journalists about what professionals should wear to work.

There are good reasons to discuss clothing choices. A businessperson's clothing accounts for a large part of the impression he or she makes on others. We make assumptions about people very quickly.

Clothing, an important form of nonverbal communication, can enhance a person's professional reputation or detract from his or her credibility. You want to send a professional message through your clothing choices.

Answer the following questions when choosing your clothing:

- **Does the clothing comply with my company's dress code?** Does your company have a dress code? Do you know what it says? Make sure your attire falls within the guidelines.

- **Will this item of clothing be appropriate for my job?** Some offices are more casual than others. Whom do you interact with on a daily basis? What is appropriate for a lawyer going to court may be very different from what's suitable for an advertising executive making a creative sales pitch. Is your usual dress so informal that you would have to upgrade it to meet with clients?

- **Is this item suitable for the event or activity that I am attending?** What do people typically wear? Think about the activity, and make an appropriate decision. Generally, you wouldn't show up at a company picnic in a business suit nor attend a formal meeting in a track suit.

- **Am I sending a professional message?** You send a message through your clothing, and you should know what it is. Do you look like you're ready to go to work or to play? Do you look like someone with whom your clients or coworkers will want to work?

Location can sometimes make a difference as to what is considered appropriate attire. If you are unsure whether something is suitable, ask someone who is likely to know. When I went to Abu Dhabi to conduct training, I asked my contact in the Middle East what would be considered proper clothing.

The bottom line: if you are unsure whether something is appropriate, choose something else.

POINT TO PONDER

The questions listed in this etiquette discussion apply whether you work for a very conservative company or a very casual one. One manager wrote after our coaching sessions ended: "I'm making headway with key people and getting noticed! Thanks for everything you've taught me. Presentation counts even in this ultracasual company."

ZUCKERBERG AND HIS HOODIE

Mark Zuckerberg always seems to wear casual clothes. And if you are as brilliant as he is, you may get away with it. But even Zuckerberg caused a stir when he showed up in a hoodie to meet with his investors. Consider the following headlines:

Zuckerberg's Hoodie a "Mark of Immaturity," Analyst Says (*Bloomberg News*, May 2012)

Is Mark Zuckerberg in over his Hoodie as Facebook CEO? (*LA Times*, August 2012)

Facebook's stock price fell after its opening IPO price. Probably not the hoodie's fault, but . . .

35. Just the FACS™, Madam: Business Clothing Essentials

People will ask me, "Can I wear this outfit?" My answer is, "I don't know unless you have paid attention to the FACS." FACS is an acronym I created to help people choose their clothing whether in a business or business casual dress work environment.

Each letter of the FACS stands for something:

- **F stands for *fit*.** Your clothing needs to fit properly. You can spend a fortune on an item, but if it is too big or too small, it isn't going to look good. One man bought shirts a size larger in order to have a fitted neck. But there was all this extra fabric hanging at his sides. He looked like he was wearing his big brother's shirt.

    Men need to have their jackets big enough so they can button and have some room, and they need their pants long enough. Pants should break at the shoe. No high waters! If men are wearing jackets, the sleeves should reach the base of their hands and just show a bit of the cuff. Shirt collars should button comfortably without pinching or leaving gaps. Some men may need to have their shirts custom-made, or they may need to buy them from specialist manufacturers who carry slim- and regular-sized shirts so their shirts fit their body.

    Women should make sure their clothing fits without the fabric bulging, which can often happen in the back of skirts or slacks when the item is too tight across the buttocks. Or sometimes, buttons can pull a shirt when it is too tight across the chest. Women need to be able to move their arms without exposing things they do not want to expose.

    When in doubt, both men and women should take their clothes to a tailor for a professional fitting.

In addition to fitting well, your clothing needs to be clean and pressed, with no holes or frays. Be cautious with permanent-press shirts. The wrinkles don't always disappear in the dryer.

POINT TO PONDER

If you lose a lot of weight, you'll need an interim wardrobe. One man lost about 60 pounds, but he simply kept adding holes to his belt. He left the extra length hanging. It looked strange and distracting.

- **A stands for *accessories.*** You need good quality accessories that complete your outfit without overpowering it. They are the finishing touches for your clothes, and they can be a good way to add color to your outfits. All accessories should be of good quality and in good condition. By coordinating with your outfit, they show you are paying attention to important details. (See the next article, Etiquette 36, for more information on accessories.)

- **C stands for *color.*** Pay attention to your color choices. Darker colors usually convey a stronger impression than lighter ones. Lighter colors may not be as powerful, but they can be very appropriate, especially in warmer climates.

  Both men and women have to be cautious with bright colors. You can shout. And you have to decide if you want to shout or not. I am NOT saying don't wear color. Just choose color carefully. A man in one of my seminars wore bright green pants and wanted my opinion. I said his slacks were not typical corporate clothing, and as a result, he would probably be referred to as "the man in the green pants."

POINT TO PONDER

A woman wore a bright yellow suit to a new-hire orientation. She was the only one not dressed in black. Two years later, she said, people still came up to her and exclaimed, "You're the one who wore the yellow suit."

I often say to those I'm coaching, "Your clothes are so loud, I can't hear you." And then I ask, "Do you want to be remembered for what you said or for what you wore?" The answer, of course, is that you want to be known for your ideas, not your clothes. Yet two years later people still remembered the woman in the yellow suit. Was this a good thing? Maybe, . . . maybe not. Answers aren't always black or white. Sometimes, they're yellow.

- ***S stands for style.*** Clothing styles can range from very formal to very informal. You generally want to be at the same level, or one step above the level, of the people with whom you are interacting. It builds your credibility.

The upshot is that you need to think about what you are doing, who is going to be there, and what they are likely to be wearing, and then you need to choose your clothes accordingly. Consider the following hierarchy:

- The business suit is still the most powerful piece of clothing for men and women.

- For women, the business suit is followed by, in descending order, the dress with a jacket, the mix-and-match jacket with skirt or slacks, the dress, and the skirt or slacks with a shirt. Then come Dockers and polo shirts for women, but these are usually not a great look for women. Jeans are very casual, but they are acceptable in the workplace if your organization approves of them and they are appropriate for your job.

- For men, the business suit is followed by, in descending order, the sport jacket and slacks, slacks and a long-sleeve shirt, slacks and a polo shirt, Dockers and a polo shirt, and a sweat suit (and note that the sweat suit is not appropriate in most business situations). As noted above for women, jeans are acceptable in appropriate circumstances.

Men seem to have an easier time with their wardrobes as they have fewer clothing choices than women.

POINT TO PONDER

It gets complicated for women. Which is more powerful: a light-colored skirt suit or a dark-colored pantsuit? The answer depends on many things: the age of the woman; the style of the outfit, whether classic or trendy; the fabric; the fit; the woman's body type; and the woman's title. Former First Lady and Secretary of State Hillary Clinton mostly wears pantsuits. Newswoman Diane Sawyer wore a skirt suit when she interviewed President Obama. You decide.

POINT TO PONDER

Know where you draw your line on what's appropriate for your workplace. A young software engineer was asked if he would wear cut-off jeans to work. He replied, "Of course not! I would wear shorts but never cutoffs! I draw my line at that." Everyone draws his or her line in a different place.

36. Accessories Are Also Part of Your Work Look

Accessories are the finishing touches for your outfit, and they can add color and style. However, while they can complete your outfit, they can also become distractions and overpower you or your clothes.

The following corporate employees caught my eye because of their use of accessories. Little things, right? What do you think?

- The supervisor who wore a bold striped shirt with suspenders, a plaid lanyard for his name tag, and a pocket protector on his shirt with numerous pens showing

- The social-media manager who had both her sunglasses and her reading glasses resting on top of her head, a scrunchie holding her hair back, and a pen resting on her ear

Here are some important suggestions about using accessories so they don't detract from your professional image or from what you are saying:

1. **If 1 is good, 10 are not better.** Do not let accessories overpower you or your outfit—like the bank manager who wore a ring on every finger. Use accessories selectively.

   Women can wear earrings, a necklace, a watch, and/or a bracelet. And if you have a lot of buttons on your outfits, you need less jewelry. General guideline: one ring per hand, one bracelet per arm. Men need to know their profession. Some men can get away with earrings and bracelets, but not all men, and not in all professions.

POINT TO PONDER

Long hanging earrings sway when you move and can mesmerize others, especially when you are making a presentation. Numerous ear piercings draw a lot of attention to your ears.

2. **Choose good quality.** Wear gold, silver, or good quality costume jewelry. Accessories should be clean and in good condition. This includes your briefcases, handbags, backpacks, ties, and scarves. Don't be like the employee who arrived at a meeting with a very old and worn briefcase. He was embarrassed when he opened his briefcase and the strap fell off. Any coats or jackets also should be clean, in good condition, and fit you properly.

3. **Be aware that an accessory can become your trademark.** If you wear a particular accessory often, you may be labeled. One man wore a different set of cufflinks every day. His colleagues started referring to him as "Link."

4. **Make sure your accessories are silent additions.** Your jewelry should not make noise. If you wear a number of bracelets, for instance, they can bump audibly against each other when you move your arms.

5. **Don't play with an accessory.** This becomes a distraction to others. Don't kept turning your ring or playing with a necktie.

6. **Be careful with the design of your phone cover.** Keep it professional. Using a cover featuring colorful polka dots or other fanciful designs can take away from your image.

7. **Take your name tag off when making a presentation.** Though not a fashion piece, the name tag becomes a distracting accessory when you are making a presentation.

8. **Choose your glasses carefully.** Brightly colored frames or unusual shapes stand out and not necessarily in a good way. According to fashion designer Vera Wang, glasses are "the most incredible

accessory. The shape of a frame . . . can change your whole appearance." Make sure it's a change you intended.

9. **No baseball caps at work.** They are very casual hats. You are at work, not a baseball game.

10. **Pay attention to your watch.** When I ask the participants in my etiquette classes to name the one accessory that they notice most on both men and women, "the watch" is the most common answer. Cell phones have replaced watches for some people, but many businesspeople still wear the timepieces because they like this accessory. And they can be status items. You can pay $25 to $25,000 or more for a watch. If you wear a watch, choose a good quality item.

37. More Questions and Answers About Business Dress

Here are some of the recent questions that I have received about dress. They confirm my belief that people are concerned about choosing the appropriate clothing for work:

Q. *In our office we have been debating the definition of dress jeans. Do you have any input on this topic that you could suggest?*
A. The term *dress jeans* is an oxymoron similar to *good junk*. And there are a lot of opinions. My definition of *dress jeans* is a pair of dark jeans that are in good condition, with no holes or frays. They are neither skintight nor big, and they are worn with a belt. Dress jeans are often dry-cleaned so they look new. Both men and women can wear them with a jacket and create a nice business casual look—if their company allows jeans.

Q. *I just read an article in Sunday's job section of the paper that said women should choose either a blue suit with white shirt, or gray. These colors convey trust, confidence, and so on. Black is too strong a color. What is your opinion about that?*
A. I am biased in my answer regarding wearing black. I wear it a lot! Yes, it is a strong color, and you can project a strong image when you wear it. You can also wear any color with black. But there's another side to my answer: since black can create a strong image, you can look severe and/or intimating if you don't pay attention to your accessories, makeup, jewelry, hair style, and/or shirt color. You also need to work to establish rapport with others. These reasons may be why the article recommends a less strong color for an interview.

Q. *I have been invited to my boss's home for dinner. What should I wear?*

A. Dinners at the boss's house, the company holiday party, or conferences are all still business events, and your clothing choices matter. You can ask the boss for the evening's dress code. If the dinner is a backyard barbecue, casual dress would be appropriate. If it's dinner on a Saturday night, it probably would be more formal. Women can usually wear a dress; men, a sport jacket.

Q. *I am attending a black-tie event sponsored by my company, and many top executives will be there. I'm wondering what is appropriate to wear. I look great in red—should I be the "lady in red"?*

A. Dressing for a black-tie event can be complicated for women. (Men usually wear a tuxedo.) Generally, women would wear a long gown, a midcalf cocktail dress, or a black tuxedo pantsuit. If you wear a dress for a black-tie event, you may be showing a little more skin than usual, but do not dress provocatively. Check with other women who are attending the party to find out what they are wearing. Red is a great color, and you will stand out if you wear it. You have to decide if that is what you want to do and how being referred to as the "lady in red" will affect your career.

38. How to Dress for a Promotion

I am being considered for a promotion and would like to up-grade my wardrobe, but don't know where to begin. We are a business casual company. Do you have any suggestions?

The woman who wanted this information was wise to consider her wardrobe as part of her career development. Clothing can help you create the look of a credible and competent professional. Here are five ways for both men and women to upgrade their wardrobes as they advance in their careers:

1. **Analyze the clothing choices of the individual who currently holds your next-level position.** What type of clothing does he or she wear? Do you think this person has a more professional appearance than you? If so, you'll want to improve your wardrobe.

2. **Look at what higher-level professionals in your organization are wearing.** You can usually model your clothing after them.

3. **Establish a relationship with an experienced personal shopper or salesperson at a good clothing store.** Explain what you wear to work now and that you would like to move your clothing up a notch. You can also work with a career coach; someone knowledgeable about professional image can give you suggestions on your wardrobe.

4. **Start wearing a jacket, sweater, or vest.** These items provide a second layer and refine your appearance.

5. **Increase the amount of money you spend on your clothing.** Spending more money on clothing will not automatically improve your

wardrobe, but often more expensive items are better quality, and that translates to an upgraded image for you.

Q. *I'm a baby boomer and surrounded by young people. What do I do to look younger?*

A. There are a number of options to try, including dyeing your hair, updating your glasses or getting contacts, whitening your teeth, and getting a new hairstyle or outfit. A contemporary wardrobe can deduct 10 years or more from a person's appearance. Some people also choose more extensive measures, like Botox or plastic surgery. If you don't know where to begin, a professional coach can help.

39. Button That Shirt and Cover That Thigh

I have been quoted both nationally (*New York Times*) and internationally (*Ottawa Citizen*) regarding my opinions about professional dress. I believe that "sexy is not a corporate look."

That's why I was disappointed a couple of years ago to see television correspondents Katty Kay of the BBC and Norah O'Donnell, formerly of MSNBC, dress rather provocatively for an appearance on the NBC-syndicated program *The Chris Matthews Show*. These public figures were guests on the show to discuss, among other things, women in the workplace. (Many other journalists dress provocatively on air also.)

Kay's shirt was open halfway down her chest, and O'Donnell's skirt had a slit that revealed most of her upper thigh.

I believe their style of clothing on this show was an unnecessary distraction. Kay and O'Donnell are both intelligent, talented, successful, and attractive women. They wouldn't be any less attractive if Kay buttoned one to two more buttons and O'Donnell closed the slit.

Kay and O'Donnell appear so confident that they may get away with dressing this way, but not all of us can. But Kay and O'Donnell are also role models for professional women everywhere, and it would be great if all role models kept this in mind when choosing their clothing.

POINTS TO PONDER

Women can be feminine without flaunting their bodies. Here are three keys to maintain an appropriate appearance in the workplace:

- **Don't reveal cleavage.** Low-cut tops that expose cleavage draw attention to your chest and are not suitable in the office. People tell me they don't know where to look when conversing with women dressed this way. I often coach women on this topic as many bosses are uncomfortable discussing it with their employees.

- **Don't overemphasize body parts.** If your blouse, sweater, slacks, or skirt are tight, your chest or your buttocks will be emphasized. If you wear strapless or spaghetti-strap sundresses or crop tops that expose your midriff, you are revealing too much skin.
- **Don't show too much leg.** Short skirts draw attention to your legs. If you sit down when wearing a short skirt, you expose even more leg. Is that where you want people to look? The general guideline is that skirts should be no higher than the top, or slightly above the top, of your knees.

Be cautious about modeling your clothing on the outfits worn by actresses on television, even if they are portraying lawyers, doctors, or other professionals. Television characters often dress provocatively. But detectives chasing after bad guys in five-inch heels are not good role models!

40. Chipped Green Nail Polish and Other Grooming Mistakes

A young woman in a new-hire program for a major financial firm asked me if her nail polish would be a problem once she started working. I responded that she would be asking her clients to trust her with their multi-million-dollar portfolios, and did she think that her chipped green nails would convey a reassuring image to her potential clients? She responded "No" and added that she thought I would say that!

You want people to focus on your abilities—not on distracting details. You do not want people noticing dandruff on your shirt, smudges on your glasses, or lipstick on your teeth.

Do not have your hair become a distraction. Women who twirl one strand of hair or men who twirl their mustache can drive others crazy! Both men and women need to have glasses that fit (it's distracting for someone to keep pushing back their glasses); clean hair; good breath (use mouthwash or breath strips); clean and groomed nails; and clean, straight, white teeth. (No picking your teeth. And see your dentist if you have missing teeth that need to be replaced.)

People also need to limit or eliminate perfume and cologne. We don't want to smell your scent after you have left the room! Plus, many people are allergic to fragrances.

No scratching or picking the nose. Do I really have to remind people about this? Unfortunately, sometimes I do.

ADDITIONAL GUIDELINES FOR MEN

- **Neat length of hair:** Know what's okay in your organization or department. You see very few ponytails in corporate America.
- **Trimmed facial hair:** Know what's okay in your organization or department. Are people wearing beards? Will you be the only one? Do you want to be?
- **No five-o'clock shadow:** You don't want to look like you just woke up.
- **Well-knotted tie:** The tie should reach the middle of the belt buckle.
- **Nose hairs clipped:** Otherwise, it's a distraction.

ADDITIONAL GUIDELINES FOR WOMEN

- **Have a hair style.** And be cautious with long hair. It can make you appear very young or sexy, or it can be a distraction in some other way. If you pull your hair back, be careful with scrunchies because they often look sloppy. Wrap a strand of your hair neatly around the band.
- **Stay away from very long nails.** Too-long nails draw a lot of attention to your hands. Be cautious with bright polish and designs on your nails. Same reason.
- **Do not allow your underwear to show.** This includes bra straps and thong underwear. And make sure your underwear fits you properly.
- **Don't overdo makeup.** Makeup is part of the corporate uniform. You look more finished if you wear a little foundation, blush, mascara, lipstick, and even eye shadow. But you don't want to look like a painted doll.
- **Avoid putting on makeup or nail polish in public.** You are at work. Attend to this grooming need in the ladies' room.

Q. *Is it okay to get a tattoo? I am concerned whether employers will hire me.*

A. Times are changing, and more and more people now sport tattoos. Yet, according to *The Patient's Guide*, tattoo removal climbed 32 percent from 2011 to 2012, and "employment reasons" was given as the motivating factor.

Here are some points to consider:

- Will your customers, clients, or bosses take a negative view of tattoos?
- If you do get a tattoo, can you conceal it easily if necessary?

Remember that even casual work environments can frown on tattoos. Consider these two workplace anecdotes:

A waitress at a casual restaurant was promoted to supervisor, and she kept talking about her new position to her customers. She commented that although her bosses would allow her to show her tattoos, she thought her customers would treat her with more respect if she covered them.

The owner of a beauty salon wouldn't hire a young hairdresser because she had tattoos and the owner thought her customers might not like them.

41. What Do 33 Miners and Your Shoes Have in Common?

Millions around the world held their breath a few years ago as 33 Chilean miners who had been trapped underground for many weeks were slowly and safely brought to the surface. It was an uplifting, exciting story, and journalists will be writing about these men and their survival for years.

Many details about their underground ordeal were really remarkable, but one item caught my attention and made me smile. When the men were preparing to leave the mine, they asked for shoe polish. I bet their loved ones didn't care whether their shoes were polished, but the miners wanted to look their best when reunited with their families.

Shoes are one of the little things that help make up your image.

Your shoe choice at work can also be significant. Others form an impression of you based upon what they see. A recruiter told me that he always notices the condition of a candidate's shoes. It tells him whether the person is paying attention to the details. Another manager wouldn't hire someone because the man wore sneakers to the interview. He believed that the candidate didn't understand the importance of the position.

Make sure your shoes are in good condition and of good quality and that they are polished and appropriate for your outfit. Additional shoe suggestions include the following:

- Good quality leather is the most professional look for both men and women.

- Flip-flops are for the beach.

- **Men:** Wear black shoes with gray, navy, or black. Wear brown shoes with tan, brown, and beige. Sock color should match your pants or shoes. Wear shoes with a tie (lace) if you are wearing a suit with a tie.

- **Women:** Heels are part of the corporate uniform, and when wearing a suit, most women wear heels. Usually, a 2½- to 3½-inch heel is appropriate. But no ultrahigh heels, please. The general guideline for shoe color is that they should be the color of your hemline or your skin color. If you add contrast to your outfit through your shoe color, people will notice your shoes more than they'll notice you. If you wear a black skirt with red shoes, where do you think people will look?

POINT TO PONDER

Heels can add height—and confidence. One woman I coached added three inches to her height. She loved being taller at work and said, "I went from five-foot-two to five-foot-five with heels. I now have a much stronger presence behind the [pharmacy] counter!"

42. Another Clothing Milestone: Have Panty Hose Disappeared from the Workplace?

It's just too hot. I have given up wearing panty hose. Is that okay?

As the summer approaches, I am often asked that question. More businesses have embraced casual dress policies, and a lot of women have stopped wearing hose.

The answer is complicated. Hosiery provides a more finished look, and you wouldn't wear a conservative business suit without hose. Yet in today's business casual environment, wearing panty hose is not always necessary.

Women need to understand the importance of projecting a professional image and then determine what's suitable for them and their workplace. Here are five items to consider:

1. **If you are wearing pants or a pantsuit to the office, your legs are not exposed.** So the question of whether or not to wear hose becomes moot.

2. **Your legs need to be in good condition to pull off not wearing hosiery.** If you have blemishes, scars, or varicose veins, panty hose will diminish their appearance. Also consider the contrast between your skin color and your clothing. A stark contrast will draw attention to your legs. Panty hose can diminish the contrast.

3. **Wearing panty hose will not fix an outfit that should never be worn to the workplace.** During the summer, people tend to be very casual

with their clothing choices. Keep belly shirts, shorts, and see-through tops at home.

4. **Is your skirt an appropriate length?** If your skirt is very short, be aware that bare legs create a very sexy and inappropriate look for the workplace.

5. **Consult your company's dress code.** Your company or job may require the wearing of hosiery, although in my experience, most companies avoid discussing this issue.

THE DUCHESS EFFECT

Don't count panty hose out just yet. Thanks to the influence of celebrity, panty hose may be making a bit of a comeback.

Since glamorous Kate Middleton wed Britain's Prince William and became the Duchess of Cambridge, she has shown a fondness for wearing nude panty hose, and her legs look spectacular. Not surprisingly, sales of her favorite shade and brands of panty hose have soared. After years of decline, sales of other brands are up as well.

The media noticed, and the resulting coverage helped spread the word farther afield. One headline proclaimed: "How Kate Middleton Saved Panty Hose with the Duchess Effect."*

The duchess has become a fashion icon for many women. If she wears panty hose, will other women continue to do so too? Stay tuned.

---

* http://www.globalpost.com/dispatches/globalpost-blogs/weird-wide-web/kate-middleton-pantyhose-the-duchess-effect.

SECTION II

EAT

During an etiquette class, a man shared that at a recent business dinner he hosted, one of his employees kept taking bites from a big piece of meat that she had on her fork. I asked him if, after seeing this behavior, he would consider promoting this woman in the future. He thought for a moment and replied, "No, I wouldn't. I couldn't have her taking clients out to dinner."

What does your dining etiquette say about you? Are you comfortable taking customers to lunch? Interviewing for a job during a meal? Knowing how to be a gracious host? Mingling with others before the meal?

Socializing with others is a way for people to get to know you *and* for you to get to know people outside of the typical work setting. You may need to eat when you are at a business meal, but you are not there for the food. You are there for business.

Knowing how to mingle with others and navigate a meal will allow you to concentrate on your guests, so you don't have to worry about which fork to use.

43. Place Settings: The Secret Language of Dining

One of my interns, a terrific student from Rowan University in South Jersey, attended an awards dinner, and she shared the following dining etiquette questions she was asked by other guests during the meal:

"Do I have your water glass?"

"What are those utensils at the top of my plate?"

"Am I eating your bread?"

My intern knew most of the answers. She is also resourceful, so when she didn't know, she unobtrusively Googled "place settings" on her smartphone under the table.

Usually, I discourage texting or cell phone use in restaurants. But reading a place setting correctly during a business meal is important—you want to spend your time connecting with the other diners, not worrying that you may be eating your neighbor's bread.

Since place settings vary depending on which restaurant you visit, knowing some general guidelines can be helpful. Here are five suggestions so you don't have to Google under the table:

1. **Use one of the following memory tricks.** They will help you to remember the correct placement of the plates, glasses, and utensils.

   - **Think of the mnemonic BMW.** It stands for bread, meal, and water, and it will remind you that your bread-and-butter plate is on the left, the meal is in the middle, and your water glass is on the right.

- **Remember your "left" and "right."** *Food* is placed to the *left* of the
  dinner plate. The words *food* and *left* each have four letters; if
  the table is set properly, your bread or salad or any other *food*
  dish, will be placed to the *left* of your dinner plate. Similarly,
  drinks are placed to the *right* of the dinner plate, and the words
  glass and *right* contain five letters. Any *glass* or *drink* will be
  placed to the *right* of the dinner plate.

    Left and *right* also work for your utensils. Your *fork* (four
  letters) goes to the *left*; your *knife* and *spoon* (five letters each)
  go to the *right*.

Q. *What do you do when the restaurant's utensils are wrapped in a napkin? I wasn't sure whether to put them all on my plate, or on the table, or on the napkin and ask for an extra napkin for my lap.*

A. In this situation, you need to help set the table. Unwrap the napkin and place the utensils on the table in the proper order: fork to the left and knife and spoon to your right. The napkin then goes on your lap.

---

2. **Learn about utensils.** Don't be like Oscar Wilde, who said, "The world was my oyster, but I used the wrong fork." The largest fork is generally the entrée fork. The salad fork is smaller. The largest spoon is usually the soup spoon. If you are having a fish course, you may see the fish knife and fork as part of the place setting. The utensils above the plate are the dessert fork and spoon, although these may sometimes be placed on either side of the plate or brought in with the dessert.

3. **As a general rule, navigate your place setting from the outside in.** Each course should have its own utensils. (In Europe and in some very formal restaurants in the United States, salad may be served *after* the main course, and the place setting would reflect this.)

4. **Don't panic if you use the wrong utensil.** When the course arrives for which you need that utensil, just ask the waiter for another.

If a dinner companion uses your utensil, quietly ask the server for another.

5. **Do what your host does.** If you don't know what to do, copy what your host is doing. It may not be right, but *you* are not wrong.

44. So Many Errors,
So Little Time to Make Them

Do you find it stressful when you are required to attend a business meeting that includes dining? Are you concerned that your manners will cause you embarrassment in front of your boss, customer, or potential employer?

You are not alone.

A participant became upset during a class I teach on dining etiquette, believing that he had made a faux pas. I had corrected the placement of his knife—the blade of his knife had been facing away from his plate instead of toward it. Before I could calm him down, another diner said, "Oh, don't worry. It's just a misdemeanor!"

I thought, "He's right." There is a continuum of severity with dining errors, from serious mistakes to minor ones. And when people understand that not every error has major consequences, it can help them relax a little when dining out for business.

THE DINING ERROR CONTINUUM™

Fatal flaw_____Minor gaffe
(Major consequences)...(Minor consequences)

A *fatal flaw* is a serious breach of dining etiquette that is easily noticed by others and might cause you to lose business, a relationship, or a job offer. These mistakes include getting drunk before or during the meal, holding your fork like a pitchfork, or talking with your mouth full. One man I heard about lost a $30 million contract because he licked his knife during a meal with a potential client.

A *minor gaffe* is a less serious breach of dining etiquette that may or may not be noticed by others. If noticed, it is unlikely that it will be held against you unless you commit a number of minor gaffes during the meal. These gaffes include using your neighbor's bread plate or putting on lipstick at the table.

Of course, what seems a minor gaffe to one person may be a fatal flaw to another. There are stories of a famous businessman—some say Henry Ford, others claim it was J. C. Penney—who decided not to hire someone because he salted his food before tasting it. Ford/Penney, so the story goes, thought this indicated that the man made assumptions without knowing all the facts.

You want to come across as a polished professional when you are dining for business. Learning as much as you can about dining etiquette makes it less likely that you'll make fatal flaws and enable you to navigate a business meal with success.

YOUR MOTHER WAS RIGHT! TABLE MANNERS FOR EVERYONE

- Turn off your cell phone before sitting down to dine, or at least put it on vibrate, and no texting under the table. You need to give your full attention to the other people at your table. And do not place your phone on the table so it won't look like you are more interested in your next call than in your dining companion.
- No gum chewing. It's not only rude to your host or hostess to be chewing gum as you are about to dine but it is also unsightly for other diners who are forced to watch you.
- No grooming at the table. This includes fixing your hair or reapplying makeup. If you must do so before leaving the restaurant, excuse yourself and go to the restroom.
- Do not push away or stack your dishes. You are not the waiter. Let the wait staff do their jobs.
- Do not use the napkin as a tissue. The napkin is for blotting the sides of your mouth; never, ever use it for blowing your nose. That's definitely a fatal flaw. If you must blow your nose, excuse yourself from the table and go to the restroom.
- Do not complain or criticize the service or food. Your complaints will appear negative, and it is an insult to your host to criticize.
- Say "please" and "thank you" when food is passed to you.

Q. *I never know when to start eating if all the meals arrive at different times. Should I wait until everyone is served, or can I go ahead when my meal arrives?*

A. Ideally, all the meals will arrive at once, and everyone can begin eating at the same time. But, alas, that doesn't always happen. When some meals arrive ahead of others, the host should say, "Please start eating so your meals won't get cold." In that case, you are free to start, but proceed slowly. With any luck, the rest of the meals will arrive before too long. Sometimes, when there is no official host, a guest who hasn't yet received his or her meal will assume this role and invite others to start.

45. Don't Kill Your Career with Your Fork

People can get nervous when dining for business. And for good reason. You don't want to blow a deal or a job offer based on your dining manners. To help people in my etiquette classes remember what not to do with their utensils, I created these four examples:

1. **Waving William:** You wave your hands around with your utensils in them when you are talking at the table. Beware—the food on the utensils may go flying toward your neighbor!

2. **Finger-Pusher Fran:** You want to eat every last bite so you use your finger to help push food onto your fork. The days of the "clean plate club" are over. If you can't get the food onto your fork without using your finger, leave it on the plate. Or eat Continental style. In this style, the knife is used to push food onto the back of the fork.

3. **Pitchfork Pete:** You make a fist around your fork when cutting your meat. You look like you are holding a pitchfork!

4. **Split-Personality Susan:** You employ both the American and Continental styles of using utensils during one meal. When eating in the American style, you cut your meat using both knife and fork, then place your knife at the top of the plate and switch the fork to the dominant hand to eat. When eating in the Continental style, you still cut your food with both knife and fork, but then you eat the meal without putting the knife down or switching the fork to the opposite hand. It's generally best to use just one style.

POINT TO PONDER

Whether you are eating American or Continental style, the handle of the fork should not be visible. Rather, it should be inside the palm of the hand, and you use your thumb and index finger to maneuver the utensil. The knife is held the same way. This is the most secure way to hold your utensils, and food is less likely to go flying.

OTHER SUGGESTIONS FOR YOUR UTENSILS

- Gently dip your soup spoon into the bowl and move it away from you to gather the soup, before you move the spoon toward you to consume the soup silently. You are less likely to spill soup on yourself this way.
- If you do not have a butter knife on your bread-and-butter plate, use your regular knife.
- Do not use your knife to cut your rolls. Break your roll in half and tear off one piece at a time, and butter the piece as you are ready to eat it.
- Place your knife and fork in the *rest position* (knife on top of plate, fork across middle of plate) to let the waiter know you are resting. Use the *finished position* (fork below the knife, diagonally across the plate) to indicate that you have finished eating.

46. Avoiding the Seven Deadly Sins of Dining

Even high-level executives and business owners have questions about dining with clients. When they entertain clients and potential clients in restaurants, they, too, want to feel comfortable and confident that they are not breaking the rules of etiquette.

When you share a meal with current or potential clients, they are not just looking to see if you slurp your soup. It's an opportunity for them to get to know you. Are you someone with whom they will be comfortable working? Are you self-assured and socially adept? If you create a welcoming and gracious atmosphere when entertaining, you will put your customers at ease and let them know you can take charge of situations.

If you invite someone to a meal, you are the host, and you want to avoid making any of these seven mistakes:

1. **Picking an inappropriate restaurant.** Match the restaurant to the guest. Don't take a very important client to a mediocre eatery. You want your guest to feel valued. Make sure the restaurant's atmosphere is conducive to talking. Get recommendations from other people, visit restaurants in advance to check them out, or check the menu on the restaurants' websites. Know if your guest has any dietary restrictions or other considerations. Make sure the restaurant offers a variety of items for the guest to consider.

   In some restaurants, if you are hosting a number of people, you can also preorder the dinner. In such instances, you usually pick three entrées ahead of time, and the restaurant prints a special menu for your guests.

2. **Forgetting to make a reservation.** You don't want to be turned away or have to wait in the lobby. Forge a relationship with a restau-

rant's staff by becoming a regular. They will know you and your preferences, address you by name, give you a better table, and in a pinch find a table for you when the restaurant is booked.

POINT TO PONDER

A salesperson told his new client he had made a 7 p.m. reservation at a popular restaurant. When they arrived, the restaurant was closed for a special party. The salesperson said sheepishly, "I thought I had made a reservation!" Either the man never made the reservation, or the restaurant messed up. Had he confirmed the reservation, this embarrassing situation could have been avoided.

3. **Not being in charge.** As host, you need to take charge of the logistics of the meal. Direct your guest to the best seat. Recommend menu items in various price ranges. Make sure your guest's order is taken first, and encourage your guest to order an appetizer and dessert if you want the meal to last longer. Also take charge of the wine selection, and base your choice on your guest's meal preference. If there are any problems at the table, such as an incorrect order, it is your responsibility to take care of them.

4. **Failing to keep the table balanced.** If your guest orders an appetizer, so should you. The same is true for dessert. You don't want to make your guest feel uncomfortable by eating a course alone.

5. **Not facilitating small talk.** As the host, you need to make sure conversation flows. Do your homework. What topics are of interest to your guest, and what is important to him or her? Ask questions to get your guest talking.

6. **Drinking too much.** You can easily say or do something you will regret if you are inebriated. If your guest has had too much to drink, make sure you arrange transportation home.

7. **Paying the bill in an awkward fashion.** If you are the host, it is your responsibility to pay the bill and add the tip unobtrusively. You

don't want to look like a cheapskate (see guidelines below). Do not make any comments about the cost of the bill. You also can arrange payment with the restaurant beforehand, and then the bill never comes to the table.

TIPPING GUIDELINES

Waiter or waitress	15–20% of the pretax bill
Sommelier (wine steward)	10–15% of the wine bill
	(20% if exceptional service)
Bartender	15–20% of the bar bill
Coat check	$1–$2 per coat

Do not take out a calculator to figure out the tip. Calculating 20 percent is usually easy for people. If the total bill was $60, I would tip $12 ($60 times 20% equals $12). You could take a dollar or two off since you don't need to tip on the tax, or if you want to give less than 20 percent. (In some parts of the United States, some waiters now expect a standard tip of 25 percent.)

Use a credit card. It makes paying the bill and adding the tip much easier, and it allows you to keep track of your expenses more readily.

Internationally, the tip is often included in the bill. You can leave a little extra if the service was good. Learn the practices of the country you plan to visit before you travel.

TIPS TO AVOID GETTING TIPSY

1. **Order a nonalcoholic beverage.** You don't want your guest to be the only one with a drink.
2. **Order a drink you don't like, and nurse that drink all evening.**
3. **Set a limit for yourself, usually one drink.** If you don't have a limit, as one young man observed, "One becomes ten very quickly!"
4. **Dilute your drink.** If you usually order bourbon on the rocks, order bourbon and water. You can also continue to weaken your drink by subtly adding water from your water glass.
5. **Have an arrangement with the bartender.** When you order scotch, you get scotch. When you order a Bloody Mary, you get tomato juice only.

47. Be My Guest:
Dinner in Three Acts

A young man was about to attend his first business dinner with potential clients. Although his boss would be the host, the young man was nervous about handling himself professionally during the meal.

I suggested that he think of the meal as a three-act play. The restaurant is the stage, and he is an actor, playing the role of the guest.

But, I told him, preparation for the show starts before he leaves home. It is important that he dress appropriately. The dinner is a business activity, and he needs to project a professional image. He also should make sure he knows the route to the restaurant, and he should leave enough travel time to get there safely and punctually, despite possible traffic snarls.

When he arrives, he needs to greet and shake hands with the other people in his group. Although he is not the official host, it is still his job to help others have a good time.

Here are the three acts that can help anyone feel more comfortable when dining for business.

First Act

During the First Act, you are setting the stage for the meal. Subtly review the place setting to make sure you're familiar with all the utensils. Place your napkin on your lap when you sit down. (The waiter may do this for you, or if there is an official host, wait until she puts the napkin on her lap and then do the same.)

Look at the menu and quickly decide what you want. How indecisive do you look if you can't make up your mind what to eat? But keep the following in mind:

- **Don't order messy meals**. My mantra is this: *Order what you know how to eat, what you like to eat, and what is easy to eat.* A business meal is not the time to experiment with new, unusual items. Nor is it the time for sloppy or difficult-to-eat dishes—stay away from spaghetti, big juicy hamburgers, and lobsters.

- **Order something in the midprice range**. If you order the most expensive item, you will look like you are taking advantage of your host. However, if your host makes recommendations, you can order any of those suggestions, though it's still better not to choose the most expensive.

POINT TO PONDER

A financial executive told me this: "I took my new employee and her husband out to dinner to welcome her to the company. The husband ordered two appetizers and the most expensive main course. I won't go out with them again."

- **Be cautious about ordering specials**. Many waiters do not mention the price when telling you their specials of the night. Specials can cost from 10 to 40 percent more than regular menu items, but you cannot comfortably ask the price of a special in a business situation.

Business talk can occur after the order is taken and before the food is served.

You also begin eating in the First Act if an appetizer, soup, or salad is being served. Each course should have its own utensils, and usually you work your way from the outside toward the plate. Hold and maneuver your utensils correctly also.

Second Act

During the Second Act, your main course is served. (At a very formal meal, a fish course may be served immediately before the main course.) Make only pleasant comments about your food. Do not criticize, and do not send your food back unless it really is inedible. Sending food back will disrupt the flow of the meal, and it may embarrass the host. Drink cautiously. Sip any wine served, and stay sober.

This is the time to talk about topics other than work. Participate in the small talk. Get to know the other people at the dinner, and let them get to know you.

Third Act

In a real play, the Third Act is the most important because this is when everything is resolved. Coffee is usually served at this point, and this is a nice time to tie up any loose ends about business. The host takes care of paying the bill.

Shake hands with, and say goodbye to, the other guests and your host. Thank all of them for a pleasant evening. Make sure you follow up promptly on any business-related promises you made to the potential clients.

48. I'm Not Eating That!
Business Meals and Dietary Concerns

Recently a young woman asked if being a vegetarian would be a problem in the business world. She was looking for work, and she was concerned about what to order when her interviews took place at restaurants.

At a previous interview, she had told the interviewer she wasn't hungry, and she didn't order anything. But by not eating, she felt excluded from the other people at the table.

She stood out, she said, but in a bad way.

Another time she ordered a vegetable plate, but it turned out to be a small plate of vegetables. The interviewer became very concerned about her meal, and he encouraged her to order more. She felt uncomfortable because his attention was being focused on her food choice and not on her skills.

I suggested that in the future, she order a double house salad as a main course if there was no vegetarian dish on the menu. A double house salad is usually served on a dinner plate, and it will often look like a main entrée. An easy-to-eat pasta dish such as vegetable tortellini is often a good choice too because many pastas are served with vegetarian sauces.

Another suggestion is to check out the restaurant's menu ahead of time to see if there is anything suitable to eat. The menu is usually on the restaurant's website. You'll appear finicky if you spend a lot of time at the table trying to decide your order.

These days, so many people are vegetarian or vegan, suffer from food allergies, or have other dietary restrictions that a lot of restaurants offer dishes designed to meet many of these special requirements. If you are not able to eat certain foods for health or religious reasons, call the restaurant in advance to find out the ingredients in an item you are interested in ordering.

Q. *My boss has invited me to lunch, and she is a vegetarian. Since she is treating, should I order a vegetarian meal to avoid offending her?*

A. Most people do not impose their dietary choices on others. Nevertheless, you can often judge what to order by the type of restaurant she chooses. If you go to a steak house, by all means you can order steak.

---

49. Treat the Wait Staff with Respect

*When I interview sales managers, I take them to lunch to see
how they treat the waiter and waitress.*

A top casino executive from Atlantic City expressed the above senti-
ment while participating in a South Jersey Chamber of Commerce
panel on networking.

His comment brings up an interesting etiquette question: If someone is not polite to the wait staff, will that person be polite to his or
her employees, colleagues, or even bosses? Many people, including
company executives, believe that how you treat a waiter reveals a lot
about your character.

I also spoke during that networking panel about etiquette. After
the meeting, a manager asked me for more information about dining and for some specific recommendations for interacting with wait
staff. I gave her the following suggestions. These behaviors are not
complicated, and diners who use them will be viewed by others as
considerate and pleasant individuals:

1. **Greet your waiter.** Say "Hello," "Good morning," or "Hi" when
   you make eye contact with the wait staff.

2. **Do not speak down to the server.** Ask for what you want politely
   and respectfully. No whistling to get your waiter's attention. Try
   to catch the person's eye, or in a polite voice say, "Waiter."

3. **Say "Thank you" when the waiter brings your food.** You can also, at
   times, acknowledge the waiter's effort with a smile or nod.

4. **If a problem occurs, be polite.** How you react to a difficult situation in a restaurant can show others how you would react in a

challenging situation at the office. Exploding at someone is not acceptable behavior.

5. **Don't punish the waiter.** Many times, when there is a problem with your service or your meal, it is not the waiter's fault. Leaving no tip is *not* okay. Speak to the manager. If you really had problems with the waiter, you could consider reducing the tip to 10 percent.

POINT TO PONDER

"A person who is nice to you, but rude to the waiter, is not a nice person." These wise words are from Dave Barry, a Pulitzer Prize–winning author, columnist, and comedian.

50. Solving the Invitation Dilemma: Kindergarten Rules

A neighbor told me that at work he goes to lunch with the same three people every day. Yet when one of the four was hosting a holiday party, he invited only two of his lunch buddies. My neighbor, who was the one not invited, was offended.

Sometimes we need to remember the basic etiquette rules that many of us learned in kindergarten about inviting classmates to your party. If you invite most of the people in a group, you need to invite everyone from the group. Or you can invite just one or two people, as long as they don't make up the majority of the group.

I am often asked a similar question by soon-to-be-married workers about inviting work friends to their weddings: "Do I need to invite my whole department?"

My answer is essentially the same. If you invite only one or two close friends, you don't have to invite the whole department. But if you invite most of the people from your department, you should invite them all. There may be exceptions, of course. For example, there may be people you rarely see since they work in a different location.

POINT TO PONDER

If you don't invite all the members of a particular group to an event, don't rub salt in the wound for those who were excluded. Avoid bringing up details of the party in the presence of colleagues who may be hurt that they weren't invited.

51. The Power of Going to Lunch

Business lunches provide opportunities for colleagues to get to know each other outside the traditional office setting.

I once had a boss who would take a different employee to lunch every month, so he could get to know his staff in a more informal setting.

Business lunches also can mend fences. Years ago, after I had experienced a particularly difficult encounter with a colleague, my mentor told me, "When the going gets tough with someone, take the person to lunch." She was right. I asked the man to lunch, and as a result, we were able to work through our differences outside of the corporate environment.

Lunches can also be acts of kindness. A colleague recently told me that when she was new to a big company, another woman from her department came up to her desk and said, "You're new here. Do you want to go to lunch?" They did go to lunch, and this simple act made the new worker's transition to the company easier. It also was the beginning of a long-term business relationship and personal friendship between the two women.

What a gracious way to help others. Why don't you ask someone to lunch when you can?

OTHER DINING OPTIONS

- **Breakfast.** This meal can be a quick and inexpensive way for colleagues to get together. Many people like meeting during this meal since it doesn't interfere with their workday.
- **Dinner.** This meal is usually more formal, takes more time, and often includes significant others. Remember that your "significant other" represents you, and his or her behavior matters. Wine is often served at dinner—drink cautiously.

- **The office cafeteria.** Be friendly to people, and don't comment negatively about the food when waiting in line. Don't cut in—even if you know somebody further up the line. Follow established cleanup protocols, such as putting your paper trash in one receptacle and your dishes in another.
- **Your office.** Occasionally, you and a colleague might get together at your desk for a quick, informal lunch. Make sure your food doesn't have any strong aromas that could annoy your office mates, and don't leave any dirty dishes or wrappers on your desk. But don't make a habit of eating only at your desk. By doing so, you are missing opportunities to get to know other colleagues and bosses, as well as opportunities to keep up with what is happening within your organization and in your field in general.

52. Wine Tales:
Don't Wave Your Hand
over the Glass

A dining scene from *Last Holiday*, a 2006 comedy with Queen Latifah, caught my attention recently as I was channel surfing. Watching people dine in formal restaurants can provide good stories for my etiquette seminars—think *Pretty Woman* and escargot flying across the room.

This fun movie was no exception. During the meal, a diner put his hand over his glass to signal that he didn't want any more wine—just as the waiter poured the wine onto his hand!

Listed below is the way to avoid a wet hand, plus additional suggestions to help you feel more comfortable dealing with wine in a restaurant:

1. **Avoid gesturing.** If you don't want any more wine, simply say "No, thank you" to the waiter.

2. **Learn about wine.** If you are the host, you are in charge of the wine selection. You can defer to your guests, but then you may end up with a $300 bottle of wine that was not in your budget. There are many books and websites with lots of information about wine. You can also take a class at an adult-education school or a wine store. The general guideline is that white wine is served with fish and poultry and red wine with meat, but there are numerous exceptions.

3. **Ask the sommelier (wine steward) for suggestions.** Most wine stewards are very knowledgeable and will be happy to pair your food choices with wine.

4. **Use my acronym LaCEST™** to help you remember the wine-tasting steps:

- ***La* stands for *label*.** The wine steward will show the host (or the person who ordered the bottle) the label from the bottle. You look at the label and nod approval that you have received the wine you ordered.

- ***C* stands for *cork*.** The wine steward opens the bottle and places the cork on the table. Check the cork. The cork shouldn't be dry and crumbly.

- ***E* stands for *examine*.** The wine steward pours a small amount of wine into your glass. Examine the appearance of the wine. Check the color and clarity.

- ***S* stands for *swirl and smell*.** Gently swirl the wine to release the aroma and then take a sniff. If you like what you smell, chances are that it will be a good bottle.

- ***T* stands for *taste*.** Take a sip and nod approval. You reject wine only if there is a problem with the wine quality. You don't send back wine if it is not to your liking. Your guests' glasses are filled first, and then yours.

  Though there are five steps involved, wine tasting is a relatively quick process. Don't turn it into a major production.

TRY THIS SUGGESTION

As the host, you can make a short, informal toast at the beginning of the meal to welcome your guests. Raise your glass and say something like, "It's really wonderful that we can all be together to celebrate the successful launch of our new product. And I would like to thank every one of you for your effort. Enjoy your meal!"

53. But You Had Lobster, and I Only Had Chicken . . .

Two couples were out to dinner. One of the couples ordered a $120 bottle of wine. They drank all the wine themselves, as the other couple wasn't drinking. When the bill came, the first couple didn't offer to pay for their wine and assumed the restaurant bill would be split in half.

People have gotten annoyed at friends, coworkers, and even relatives when they are dining together and one party orders significantly more costly items than the other and then doesn't offer to contribute more to the bill. One colleague told me that she and her husband will not dine out with another couple again because this couple always orders the most expensive items on the menu and expects them to share the costs.

I am often asked about sharing bills at restaurants. At a business meal, of course, the host would pay the bill. But since many people socialize with coworkers outside of work, here are some suggestions for dining with others and splitting the bill:

1. **Pay attention.** I don't believe that most people are trying to take advantage of others. They simply aren't paying attention. Make a mental note of the cost of the items and the number of courses you order, and compare them with what the other diners order. But you don't want to be a nitpicker. A $16 entrée is similar to a $19 entrée, but not a $32 entrée. Also, there is a difference if you order an appetizer, salad, main course, coffee, and dessert, and everyone else orders just entrées and desserts. This applies to drinks too.

2. **Offer to pay more if you ordered more expensive items than the rest of the group.** Calculate quickly your additional share—it doesn't

have to be exact to the penny! The other couple doesn't have to accept your offer, but what is important is that you offered. Often, couples who socialize frequently have a tacit understanding that over time, the cost differences balance out between them.

3. **Separate checks aren't always a solution.** They can make your meal seem more like a business arrangement than a friendly outing with colleagues. And some restaurants don't want to provide them, especially when they are busy.

4. **Let it go, or say something.** If the other person's share is significantly more than yours and he or she doesn't offer to contribute more, you can choose to speak up politely. When you look at the bill, you can say something like, "Your share is actually more than half. Why don't you pick up the tip?" People have told me that they would never feel comfortable saying something; they would rather just stop seeing the person. I respond that if they are ready to end a relationship over the issue, what do they have to lose by saying something?

Q. *If a Groupon or other discount coupon is used for a business meal, what amount gets submitted to your company for reimbursement?*

A. First of all, be cautious if using a coupon when dining for business. You don't want to convey to your client that he or she is a "discount date." If you do use a coupon, try to be discreet. Seek reimbursement for the amount you actually paid for the meal, plus whatever you paid for the discount coupon. You may need to include a copy of the coupon for reimbursement. Also, calculate the waiter's tip based on the precoupon amount of the bill.

---

54. A Table for One? Yes, You Can!

I returned from giving a seminar in Las Vegas, and I mentioned to a colleague that I had eaten by myself at a really nice restaurant. She replied that when she travels, she orders room service because she is uncomfortable dining alone.

Many business travelers take similar steps to avoid eating by themselves in restaurants. Yet dining solo doesn't have to be unpleasant or awkward. Here are four tips to help you enjoy your food and your own company when dining alone:

1. **Pick a nice restaurant.** Ask for a recommendation from the hotel concierge, a colleague, or your client. Ask about any special food that the restaurant might serve, especially any local delicacy. I tried walleye fish when I was in Minnesota to give a seminar. There may be an excellent restaurant in your hotel. If you plan to leave the hotel to dine, make sure you get good directions so that you can get to the restaurant and back safely.

2. **Relax and enjoy your dining experience.** Do not be embarrassed because you are alone. Take pleasure in your own thoughts, the time away from the hustle of your workday, and good food. Put your phone on vibrate, and if you must use your phone, speak in a quiet, conversational voice that does not disturb others. (Some good restaurants ask that you do not use cell phones at all.) You can read a book while waiting for your food, but make sure your electronic devices (Kindle, iPad, and the like) do not make any noise.

3. **Don't barge into other people's conversations.** However, sometimes it may be appropriate to comment to other diners near you. If you have made eye contact, and they seem receptive, you may

enjoy some pleasantries with them. You never know whom you may meet.

4. **Practice good dining etiquette.** Your table manners still matter. You don't want to be a distraction to others. Tip generously. When I receive excellent service, I show my appreciation with a 25 percent tip.

DINING OVERSEAS: DON'T MAKE THESE MISTAKES

1. **Don't refuse to try different and unusual foods.** Always try a little. If you reject the food, it may be interpreted as rejecting your host. And don't comment negatively on any unusual customs you may encounter. In a very nice French restaurant, I sat next to another diner and his dog.

2. **Don't show disdain for different utensils.** Depending where you are in the world, you may not use a knife and fork. In some cultures, you may use chopsticks or your fingers. Enjoy the novel experience. I shared a meal with one of my students in Abu Dhabi and ate with my fingers. It was the highlight of my visit.

3. **Don't ignore local customs regarding the consumption of liquor.** In many European countries, wine is an important component of the meal, and you will be encouraged to drink. In many Middle Eastern countries, however, drinking liquor is against the religion, and visitors should adhere to this ban. No matter where you are in the world, if you choose to drink alcohol, be smart about it and stay sober.

55. Are There Any Manners
for a Food Fight?

This unlikely question was asked when I volunteered to teach dining to my son's fourth-grade Boy Scout troop. It's the only time I can remember that I was at a total loss for words—and it may be the reason my business is oriented to corporations!

Usually, I teach adults, but I recently agreed to take a colleague's 12-year-old daughter to lunch at a white-tablecloth restaurant. The young woman's parents wanted their child to brush up on her table manners before her upcoming Bat Mitzvah.

As I prepared for this atypical teaching activity, I created a number of steps that anyone could use to take a friend's or colleague's child for a dress-up lunch or dinner. It's a gift that makes memories to last a lifetime—and excellent training for the next generation of executives.

The following are my seven steps for a successful Take a Child to Lunch activity:

1. **Do not include the parents.** It's amazing how well behaved some children can be when their parents are not around. I know—as a child, my son was a great guest, but he could be a handful at home. Let the parents know this is a private, unique activity for their child and you.

2. **Choose a nice restaurant.** Pick a place that will be special for the child. Make a reservation. Make sure the atmosphere is conducive to talking. Tell the child that you will be going to a nice restaurant and that he or she should be dressed appropriately.

3. **Let the child set the parameters.** Ask the child how much he or she knows about table manners, based on a 1-to-5 scale, 5 being the best. Also, ask how much the child wants to learn. My guest

said she was a 1 and wanted to become a 5. As a result, she was giving me permission to give her feedback. But remember that all feedback must be given in a positive way.

4. **Order a three- or four-course meal.** You want the child to experience different courses. Possible choices include an appetizer, soup, salad, entrée, and dessert.

5. **Don't overwhelm.** Concentrate on just three or four key learning points, such as choosing items from the menu, understanding the place settings, and holding and using the knife, fork, and spoon correctly. Young people usually enjoy learning the memory trick BMW (bread, meal, water) to remind them that their bread-and-butter plate is on the left and their water glass is on the right.

6. **Make the experience fun.** Make pleasant conversation, and use some amusing, even gross, stories to emphasize the importance of manners. Examples include the woman who clipped her fingernails at the table, the man who licked his dessert plate clean, or the young man who tucked the tablecloth into his waistband when he didn't have a napkin and pulled all the dishes from the table when he went to the restroom.

7. **Discuss the importance of thank you notes.** The young person can use either email or stationery. My young woman sent a printed note card that said, "Thank you for teaching me proper manners. I had a lot of fun."

56. Lots of Dining Questions . . .
No Shortage of Answers

People think that dining is a simple activity—we all eat, after all—but it's astonishing how many questions it generates. Not only in seminars but through email and on Facebook, I probably get more questions on dining etiquette than on any other topic I teach.

Below are some questions that come up often, in one variation or another:

Q. *At a breakfast meeting recently, a woman left the table briefly and placed her napkin on the table—and part of it fell into my coffee cup! This can't be right. Where should she have placed her napkin?*
A. When you leave the table temporarily, you place your napkin on your chair. Other diners don't want to see your dirty napkin—nor do they want it to fall into their food or drink.

Q. *I took a client out for dinner, and it took the waiter a long time to come to our table to take our order. It was a really nice restaurant, known for its service. How should I have let the waiter know I was ready to order?*
A. Since you say it was a really nice restaurant, it is possible that you didn't give a signal to the waiter that you were ready to order. A signal, you say. What signal? The signal is closing your menu. Don't feel bad if you were unaware. One man told me, "For 30 years I have been getting upset in restaurants because I didn't know the signal!" You can also catch the waiter's eye and give a little nod to indicate you are ready.

Q. *How do I tell someone that he has spinach in his teeth?*
A. The key is that you do need to say something. You are saving the person further embarrassment. But don't broadcast the news. You should tell the person privately and quietly. This can be somewhat nerve-racking for the person who has to do the telling, but remember that you are giving the person information that he can fix right away. You simply describe the situation: "Tom, there is spinach between your teeth." The same applies to any potentially embarrassing situation.

Q. *Is it okay to request a doggie bag?*
A. No. You are there for business, not for the leftovers. Doggie bags are okay for family dinners but not during professional occasions.

Q. *The CEO of my company invited me to lunch to celebrate a successful product launch. He told me to "pick somewhere in the city where you've been wanting to eat." Now that sounds like an open invitation to splurge, but it left me wondering what kind of place I should choose? I'm guessing he's footing the bill (is that implied?), but should I choose a restaurant that is upscale, midrange, or downscale?*
A. I would choose a nice upscale restaurant with a variety of prices on the menu. It should not be the most expensive restaurant in town. Since the CEO did the inviting, he will be the host and should be picking up the bill. Enjoy your meal!

57. Champagne, Your Career, and the Holiday Party

My list of holiday party guidelines has been published by many news organizations, for one practical reason: the suggestions encourage employees to enjoy holiday celebrations without making career-damaging mistakes.

Here are my seven guidelines for office party success:

1. **Remember to RSVP.** Let people know that you will attend. And if you cannot go, provide a very good reason. The party is a business activity, and you are expected to participate. Also, arrive on time.

2. **Dress appropriately.** It may be a celebration, but your attire needs to be suitable for a business social event, not a nightclub.

3. **Prepare your significant other.** Let him or her know what to expect at the party, discreetly point out your supervisors or bosses, and warn of any problem people or topics of conversation to be avoided—politely and graciously, of course.

4. **Schmooze with people.** Keep the conversation upbeat. Complaining about the company or the economy is a downer. Parties allow you to mingle with people from different areas of the company. Talk to people you know *and* to those you don't know. The person you meet at the party may turn out to be the person who interviews you for your next job.

5. **Don't post negative opinions about the party on your social-media sites.** Tweeting that you don't want to attend isn't appropriate. Also, do not post on social media, during or after the event, any photos or comments that feature someone's unbecoming behavior.

6. **Do not get drunk**. Holiday parties sometimes have a lot of liquor flowing. It's a celebration—why not have a few drinks, right? Wrong! People have lost their jobs for the sake of those "few drinks"—it is easy to do something outrageous when you've had too much to drink. (See Etiquette 46, "Tips to Avoid Getting Tipsy.")

7. **Don't sneak out.** Say "Goodbye" and "Thank you" to the host or party organizers. Usually, you will want to send a thank you note also.

The bottom line is that your behavior always matters. All of these suggestions apply to other business social events too, including dinner at the boss's home, a retirement party, or someone's wedding or birthday celebration.

POINT TO PONDER

People often feel compelled to mark holidays by wearing costumes or accessories to celebrate the theme of the holiday. If you must do this, do so discreetly. And on Halloween, dress up at work only if others do—but don't dress outrageously.

58. I'm Too Embarrassed to Go Alone

A seminar participant told me she wasn't going to a networking dinner meeting because she didn't have anyone to go with her. I replied that by not attending the dinner, she was missing an opportunity to meet new people and to learn from the event.

I also commented that many people attend business social activities by themselves. Some prefer to do so because it enables them to interact with more people.

In today's world, many businesspeople feel that it is easier to talk to people on social-media sites or by texting them. Yet by not venturing out and socializing in person, they are missing opportunities to learn from others and to meet new people. The more you practice going to events on your own, the more comfortable you will be.

Here are some suggestions to help you overcome your reluctance to attend dinner meetings solo:

- **Identify your purpose before you go.** Is it to meet a particular person? Hear the latest from a speaker? Find out about any job openings? Catch up with colleagues? Add people to your network? Knowing your purpose can help to keep you focused on achieving your objective, and that will make you less self-conscious.

- **Walk into a room as though you belong there.** Because you do! After you enter, stand to the side and get your bearings. Is there an official host or receiving line that you need to approach? Do you need to sign in? Where's the food and drink? Do you see someone you know? Do you need to find your table or get a seat? Identify an area where you want to begin and walk confidently to it.

- **Know that others are uncomfortable also.** You are not alone. Many people feel ill at ease when attending business social events. The secret is not to let others know that you are uncomfortable. Look approachable. Don't stand with your arms crossed and a stern look on your face. Make eye contact with others, and have a pleasant facial expression.

- **Don't attach yourself to one person.** If you see someone you know, by all means talk to the person. But you also want to meet new people. Circulate and introduce yourself to others.

- **Join a table.** Pick a table that has a few people already seated. When you go to sit down, you can ask someone at the table, "Do you mind if I join you?" Most often the person will encourage you to sit down. You should reply with a quick "Thanks," then introduce yourself to that person and the others at the table. Conversation usually follows.

POINT TO PONDER

You may be the only one from your company at a conference, but you can be sure your boss or colleagues will find out about your behavior—especially if it is less than stellar. Remember, you are still at work even if you are away from the office.

59. Etiquette Niceties When Visiting Others

A colleague told me that when her son's girlfriend was visiting, she asked the girlfriend to help make the salad for dinner. The young woman said "No." My colleague was stunned by the response, and she made the salad herself.

I couldn't believe that someone would refuse to help in such a situation, but my colleague assured me that she wasn't making up the incident.

The story made me realize that in today's fast-paced world, there are businesspeople who either don't know or have forgotten the etiquette niceties required when visiting the homes of others. When traveling for your company, you may be invited for a meal or an overnight stay at the home of a colleague or client, or you may be invited for a weekend at a colleague's beach house. Not behaving appropriately could be damaging to these relationships or your career. So here's a brief refresher on the general guidelines:

- **Remember you are a guest.** It is not your home. Pay attention to how others live. Putting your feet on the coffee table in your family room may be okay, but it may not be okay in your host's family room.

- **Bring a small gift.** It's a thoughtful way to show that you appreciate the kindness of your host. A colleague joined me at the beach for the day. She brought as a gift a small candle set, which is still displayed on the mantel. If you are staying a few days with someone, buying your host dinner and/or paying for groceries is very considerate.

- **Offer to help.** The host shouldn't wait on you. Offer to help with preparing meals and/or organizing any activities.

- **Clean up after yourself.** Your visit shouldn't make more work for your host.

- **Say thank you; send a note.** When leaving, say thank you and follow up with a handwritten or email note. My son's friend recently sent a wonderful handwritten thank you note after her visit. She can visit again anytime.

═SECTION III═
TWEET

The ways in which people communicate are changing rapidly. In the digital workplace, electronic interactions—text messages, Facebook posts, tweets, video chats, blog commentaries, email messages—are used to convey information as much as, or more than, in person discussions, phone calls, and written correspondence.

These newer kinds of communication allow people to interact with others quickly and easily and to share news efficiently with more people than ever before.

The possibilities offered by each new technological advance seem endless. One young woman gushed during a seminar: "My new phone is everything. You can text, email, call, tweet, or post . . . everything!"

But it cannot protect users from blunders. As with all things new, there is a learning curve.

It takes time to understand how to use the new tools politely and how to communicate effectively with them in the workplace. And whether you are using your smartphone to text a colleague from the local coffee shop, your computer in your cubicle to tweet your followers, or the traditional office phone to call a customer, you need to remember the basics:

1. **Be professional.** Know what image you are projecting. You don't want to say or do anything that might prompt others to question your competence or that might negatively impact your career.

2. **Pay attention.** People have made all sorts of mistakes by being care-less with the technology. One employee for an advertising agency that had a huge contract with a car company tweeted negative things about Detroit drivers. He thought he was tweeting on his personal account, but he was on the company's. He was fired, and his company lost the contract with the car company.

3. **Learn the preferred style of communication of your customers, clients, bosses, and colleagues, and adjust your style to meet theirs, whenever possible.** This means that if someone mostly emails you, email that person when you want to contact him or her. If the person texts you, text the person. And so on.

60. Man, That's Rude!
Five Don'ts for All Phones

In an episode of the television hit The Big Bang Theory, the star, Sheldon, is having trouble getting in contact with his girlfriend, and he says to his roommate, "I've tried email, video chat, tweeting her, posting on her Facebook wall, texting her . . . nothing!"

His roommate asks, "Did you try calling her on the telephone?"

Sheldon replies, "Ah, the telephone."

As he starts to dial her number, he says to his roommate, "In your own simple way, you may be the wisest of us all."

Talking to someone on the phone is still an important way to communicate in business: you can get immediate feedback or acknowledgment, you can eliminate the back-and-forth of texts and emails, and you can use vocal expression to enhance your message. It also allows more in-depth discussion. Although she usually emails or texts me, my former social-media intern will call me when she needs to discuss something as important as her next career move.

However, it is just as easy to be rude or to offend someone inadvertently on the phone as it is on any other electronic device. Whether you are tethered to a landline or using a smartphone, here are five suggestions for using phones in business:

1. **Use a greeting, and give your name when answering the phone.** Say "Hello" or "Good morning," and say your full name, rather than just your first name. Using only your last name can sound too abrupt. You also need to include a verb—as in, "This is Brittany Jones speaking" or "This is Jake Jones." And when you place a

call, identify yourself with your full name again: "Good morning. This is Colby Bennett. Is Caitlyn Jones available?"

2. **Don't answer your telephone while meeting with someone.** If you answer a call, you are indicating to the person with whom you are meeting that the person on the phone is more important. And sometimes you don't even know who is calling. If you *really* have to answer the phone during the meeting—if your boss is calling from overseas, for example—you should tell the person in advance that you are expecting a really important call. If you forget to mention it beforehand, you can say, "I have to answer this" and then briefly explain before taking the call.

TRY THIS SUGGESTION

If you are in the room when the person with whom you are meeting answers a call, instead of just sitting there and feeling awkward, you can nonverbally signal that you will step outside for a moment. Then do so.

3. **Have a professional message on your voice mail.** Saying "Hey, you've reached Jen; you know the drill" is not okay. Let people know whom they have reached, give your full name, and say that you will return the call. If you regularly update your message, make sure the message is current. Do not have distracting background noise.

4. **Apologize if you dial a wrong number.** A simple "I'm sorry, I've dialed the wrong number" is all that's needed. Technology allows people to identify a caller's number, and you don't want the person calling you back and asking, "Why did you hang up on me?"

5. **Don't disturb others when putting your phone on speaker.** When your phone is on speaker, it's easy for others to hear your conversation. Do you want the details of your conversations audible to all? If you must use the speaker mode to include others in the call, make sure you immediately let people at the other end know who is in the room with you. There are many horror stories of callers not being told, and then criticizing someone in the room.

61. Man, That's Really Rude!
Tips for Cell Phone Users Only

While having breakfast at a diner in New Mexico, I noticed two men who had finished breakfast and had waited quite a while for the overworked waitress to give them a check. Finally, one guy pulled out his cell phone and called the restaurant. When the waitress answered the phone, he asked her if they could please get their check. It worked. The waitress was laughing when she promptly brought them the check.

A participant in one of my seminars recounted this story of an enterprising use of a cell phone. As almost everyone knows, now that business phone use is not confined to the office, there are many more ways to use your cell phone . . . and more ways to blunder. Here are just a few ways in which your cell phone behavior may make people regard you as impolite:

1. **Placing your phone on the table when meeting with others.** Don't do this. *Please* don't do this! Some people have even been known to put both of their phones on the table. How does this look to the people with whom they are meeting? That the phone fanatics are *so* ready to drop them and connect with someone else.

POINT TO PONDER

An article in the July 2012 issue of the *Journal of Social and Personal Relationships* stated that the presence of a mobile phone influences face-to-face conversation and that it can have negative effects on closeness, connection, and conversation quality.

2. **Using a Bluetooth headset in the office.** It looks like a cockroach in your ear. (Yes, I do have strong opinions about this.) I am not talking about the hands-free headset that receptionists use. I am talking about the headsets all too often worn by people who are walking around the office and talking, and you think they are talking to themselves. Or even worse, you think they are talking to you.

3. **Speaking too loudly.** People still need to be reminded to speak in a quiet, conversational voice. If the people around you are glaring at you, chances are, you need to lower your voice.

4. **Forgetting to put your phone on vibrate.** It is easy to forget, which is why theaters and religious services still issue reminders. The vibrate buttons in today's phones are easily activated and deactivated.

Q. *My company would allow me to use my personal smartphone as my work phone too. Should I do this?*

A. It is easier to have only one phone, but keep in mind that if you do this, you will never get away from your work. One young financial analyst told me, "When I had a company phone, I was able it leave it at home when I went out at night. Now, I am always connected to work." For some, this may be a good thing; for others, not so much.

---

62. Have a Normal Ring, Please!

I like music. I really do. Yet I believe businesspeople need to be careful with the songs they choose as their ring tones. You don't want to have a ring tone that startles others.

Consider these examples:

In the middle of an important pitch for business, "Dancing Queen," a very lively and energetic song from ABBA, started playing—and kept playing. The cell phone's owner, who was trying to sell her services, wasn't able to find the phone because it was buried in her purse. She was embarrassed.

The ringing notes of Handel's "Hallelujah" chorus let a man know he was receiving one of his infrequent calls from his son. His coworkers were startled every time it happened.

Halfway through a business speech, "Don't You Wish Your Girlfriend Was Hot Like Me?" started playing loudly from the speaker's pocket, causing his audience to start laughing. The man had borrowed his daughter's phone and didn't know her ring tone. As he frantically tried to turn off the phone, the audience laughed even more.

(The man hadn't chosen this ring tone, of course—but he had neglected to mute the phone before making his presentation.)

"Normal" doesn't mean the old telephone ring tone; in fact, the default ring tone on the iPhone is percussive marimba music. In addition to marimba, I hear a lot of xylophone music on phones. Choose, buy, or create a ring tone that won't shock or alarm people.

But please stay away from the "bark" or "duck" tones. They really can cause people to jump.

Any ring tone, however, can be an embarrassment in the wrong situation. One neglectful iPhone owner made national headlines when his marimba music began competing with Gustav Mahler's Ninth Symphony at New York's Lincoln Center.

Maestro Alan Gilbert, conducting the New York Philharmonic, first requested that the offending noise be turned off. When it didn't cease quickly enough, Gilbert stopped the orchestra until the phone was silenced—and the audience applauded his action.

TRY THIS SUGGESTION

One pharmacy student told me during a class when we discussed ring tones: "I keep my phone on vibrate so I don't have to worry about my ring tone!"

63. Don't Ruin Ur Career: Texting Guidelines

I can't believe we lost the contract because of the vice president. He shows up late and texts during the sales meeting. The potential client was furious and went elsewhere. —Salesperson at a technology company

Texting can be an unobtrusive way to contact someone, and it can be a fast and informal way to exchange information. Texting allows you to "talk" on your phone without saying a word. Yet, if you are texting colleagues, bosses, employees, customers, or vendors, you want to be professional.

Follow these suggestions so your texting is suitable for business:

1. **Be careful with abbreviations**. Using shortcuts has become more common in the business world, but make sure it's appropriate for *u* to be that informal. Plus, the receiver of the text needs to know the meaning of the abbreviations. A colleague received the text message "np" after thanking someone for his help. It took him a few moments to figure out that "np" meant "no problem."

2. **Don't text under the table during a meeting or presentation**. It's noticeable, and it is distracting to the speaker as well as to the other people in the room. This use of the phone has been a hard habit for people to break. People think that since the phone is under the table, it's not visible. What's the harm? The truth is that the phone may not be visible, but the body language of looking down and the movement of the fingers are very revealing.

   If you don't want people to text when you speak, don't text when they do. And if that doesn't persuade you, maybe this will:

an intern at a large company texted during meetings and was let go as a result.

3. **Don't use text shortcuts when you are emailing from your phone.** It is very easy to forget that you are emailing, not texting, since you can use the same keyboard for both. One woman emailed her thank you note after a job interview from her phone, and she inadvertently used text shortcuts. She didn't get the job as a result.

4. **Be aware of your tone.** Your text may sound harsher than you intend.

5. **Choose your content carefully.** It's hard to have a meaningful discussion via text message. You especially don't want to apologize in a text. People prefer a personal discussion. If that is not possible, the telephone is the next best alternative. Also, don't give negative feedback or quit your job in a text. In both cases, speak to the person concerned. Even if you are leaving a company, you don't want to burn your bridges—you may need a reference in the future. But you can send good news via text. This way the person receives the information immediately.

POINT TO PONDER

When former Titans quarterback Vince Young texted an apology to his coach Jeff Fisher, it made the headlines—but not always in a positive way. Among the media comments:

- Titans' Fisher Not Impressed with Texted Apology from Young
- Former Titans QB Offers Great Apology . . . in the Worst Format Possible
- Young Texted Apology, Says Fisher, Who'd Prefer Face-to-Face

6. **Be cautious if changing meeting times or venues in a text.** The potential attendees may not check their phones in time. Know your colleagues. Older workers may not look at their phones as often as their younger counterparts.

7. **Check for accuracy when using the voice-to-text feature.** Smartphones allow you to speak your message, which the phone then converts to text. But a lot can be lost in the translation. Make sure that what you said is what is showing as text, *before* you hit the send button.

8. **Ignore AutoCorrect at your peril.** Pay attention when typing. Auto-Correct's changes are not always correct. I thought I had responded to a vendor "NP" ("no problem") when she told me she was running late, but my phone AutoCorrected and the vendor received a text that said "NO." People have so many examples of funny AutoCorrects that television's *The Ellen Show* has a segment titled "Clumsy Thumbsy" that highlights these messages. AutoCorrect can be switched off, but if you are a poor speller, AutoCorrect can be a lifesaver.

9. **Don't drink and text.** You can easily say something you will regret later.

POINT TO PONDER

At least two managers—one at a liquor store, another at a movie theater—have banned their employees from texting during working hours. The texting was causing the employees to be distracted, and as a result, they were careless with the cash drawer.

64. Is *Anyone* Listening to Voice Mail?

"Don't leave me voice mail messages. I don't listen to them anymore," my college-bound son proclaimed a few years ago. He added, "I can see that you called, and I'll call you back."

As I thought about my son's statement, I realized that I don't always listen to messages left on my smartphone. When I was giving a seminar recently, my husband left a message. At break, I returned his call and nervously asked, "Is everything okay?"

He responded, "Didn't you listen to my message?"

I answered truthfully, "No, I didn't."

"Isn't that a breach of etiquette?" he questioned. "If I take the time to leave a message, shouldn't you take the time to listen?" (*Ouch!* He has lived with me too long.) Since my husband rarely contacts me at work, I was worried that something bad had happened. I thought that calling him back, instead of listening to the message, was a faster response.

Saving time is one of the major reasons people give for not listening to their messages. Other reasons include that some callers leave messages that are too long or they never give the reason for the call. Some people simply find it very quick and easy to return calls on their smartphones, without bothering to listen first to any message.

But whether you leave messages for others or you are tempted to ignore messages left for you, consider these etiquette guidelines:

- **Make sure you listen to any messages left by clients, customers, or your boss.** They will expect you to listen to their messages to gain information or respond to their requests. If you don't, you may be viewed as unresponsive, or you could find yourself in an embarrassing situation. Or you may simply be left out of the loop in the future.

- **Don't become known as long-winded.** Leave messages that recipients will listen to. Say what you have to say succinctly. Speak clearly, and let the person know why you called. And if you leave your number, say the numbers slowly. It drives people crazy when they have to replay the message numerous times in order to get the right numbers.

- **Know the informal protocols among your colleagues.** Do they leave messages? Or like my son, do they just expect you to see that they called, which is enough for you to know to call them back?

- **Don't play games.** One manager I know of tells employees that he doesn't listen to their messages, even though he does. He believes that some employees leave messages to avoid difficult conversations. And he wants to force them to have the discussion.

    There may be times when you can ignore a message and simply call back. I usually don't listen to my sisters' messages. I know they are only going to say, "Call me!"

Q. *Is it okay to let my caller know that I know he or she is calling?*

A. No, for two reasons. One, you may be wrong. Someone else may be using the person's phone. This is not as likely with cell phones, but offices still use landlines. And the second reason is that you will appear to be screening your calls. Of course, there are always exceptions. If you know someone very well and you are always calling each other, you could answer, "Yes, Tom . . ."

---

65. The Etiquette of Talking *to* Your Phone

When my book *The Jerk with the Cell Phone* (Marlowe & Company) was published nearly a decade ago, etiquette guidelines for talking *to* your phone were not relevant. The world has changed a lot in that time, and guidelines are now needed to help people talk politely *to* their phones in public.

I asked Apple's Siri for her opinion. My question was this: "What are the etiquette suggestions for talking *to* your phone?" Alas, she didn't have an answer and referred me to the Internet.

Here are my suggestions for talking *to* your phone politely:

- **Be considerate of others.** This is the main etiquette suggestion to keep in mind, and of course, it is applicable to all types of phones. When you are in public, you are sharing space with others, and your use of your phone should never disturb others. People sometimes forget where they are, or they don't pay attention to their surroundings.

- **Don't keep trying.** If Siri doesn't understand your request, try alternative wording. Simply talking louder won't change her response. After two or three failed attempts, use the Internet.

- **Don't yell.** Use a quiet, conversational voice. Barking commands to a phone in public is disruptive and annoying to others.

- **Respect quiet zones.** If talking *on* your phone is not allowed, neither is talking *to* your phone.

- **Be aware of your surroundings.** You never know who is listening. People eavesdrop. Don't ask a question if you suspect the answer may give away information you don't want others to know.

TELECONFERENCING

Q. *I hate teleconferencing. I find it so difficult to voice my opinion. What do I do?*

A. You are not alone—I get a lot of complaints about teleconferencing. Here are some suggestions to get your voice heard:

- **Be prepared.** Have notes. If you consult them, no one will know, and it will be easier to interject your comments when you know what you want to say.
- **Take the initiative.** Speak up early. The sooner you join in, the sooner you become part of the discussion. Say your name—"This is Joyce Star"—before you start talking. Not everyone will recognize the sound of your voice.
- **Speak loudly.** You want what you say to register on others. Have good posture when on the line. It will affect your voice.
- **Learn to interrupt politely.** I know that interrupting is usually an annoying speaking habit, but in some circumstances, if you don't interrupt, you will never get heard.
- **Arrange for a strong facilitator if you can.** This person can make sure that the agenda is followed and that everyone gets to contribute.

66. Are Facebook . . . Twitter . . . *Any* Social Media Necessary?

Television continues to poke fun at social media. Consider the following:

- Max (Kat Dennings), one of the two stars of the television show *Two Broke Girls*, said in the season opener in October 2012: "Twitter is stupid. And Instagram is Twitter for people who can't read."

- Betty White hosted *Saturday Night Live* in 2010 for the first time, thanks to fan-page demand on Facebook that went viral. During her opening monologue on SNL, White thanked Facebook as only she could: "I really have to thank Facebook," the longtime—and long-lived—television star told her audience. "When I first heard about the campaign to get me to host SNL, I didn't know what Facebook was, and now that I do know what it is, I have to say, it sounds like a huge waste of time."

Is Facebook a waste of time? Is Twitter stupid? What about Linke-dIn? YouTube? Pinterest? Does social media provide business opportunities for you—or just opportunities to get into trouble?

Social media's impact on the world has been demonstrated time and again, from its role in revolutions to political elections. Closer to home, countless businesses and organizations have made social media an integral part of their marketing efforts as an invaluable way to connect with their customers. On the other hand, people have lost their jobs based on their social-media use. One article I saw was titled "The Top 10 Tweets to Get You Fired."

There are many social-media platforms available, and new ones seem to be appearing all the time. Follow these three general suggestions to ensure that social media helps, rather than hurts, you and your career:

- **Stay up-to-date**. Know what's going on in the social-media world. Read about social media, talk to others about it, and try out different platforms for yourself. You may appear out of touch if you don't.

- **Know what your customers and clients are doing.** This knowledge can help you establish relationships with them. Know what your competition is doing. If your competition is tweeting, maybe you should be doing so too.

- **Provide value**. Have a strategy for your postings. Mine is to have my posts provide business etiquette and career suggestions to help people realize their potential. One of my colleagues recently tweeted about what she had for dinner. Do her followers really want this information?

Is social-media networking a waste of time? I don't think so. It landed Betty White on *Saturday Night Live*, after all. And it got huge laughs on the season opener of *Two Broke Girls*. Social media is undeniably here to stay. Find out what it can do for you.

67. Costly Mistakes with Tweets, Posts, and Requests

I rarely have to remind people anymore to turn off their cell phones in meetings, to avoid all caps in emails, or to speak slowly when leaving a phone number on voice mail. These technologies have been around for a while, and most people have adjusted.

Yet, as newer ways of connecting appear in the workplace, people initially make all sorts of mistakes that can affect their jobs or careers. Inevitably, interactions on Facebook, Twitter, and YouTube have caused some to stumble.

It is only over time, as etiquette experts weigh in and people learn from their mistakes, that professionals start using new tools more effectively and politely. In the meantime, avoid these costly blunders:

1. **Criticizing your employer.** One woman posted on her Facebook page, "Attending another stupid work meeting. Can't wait to get to the bars!" Despite many warnings about the pitfalls of doing so, people are still posting negative comments about their company or boss on social-networking sites. You can be reprimanded or fired because of it. Why would you bite the hand that feeds you?

2. **Posting offensive photos and videos on any social-media site.** Do you really want to risk losing your job over a post? People mistakenly think they are being funny, but it's not funny. It's rude. Two employees at Domino's Pizza lost their jobs after posting a video of themselves on YouTube doing unmentionable things to a pizza. This illustration is one that Mashable used in an article entitled "10 People Who Lost Jobs over Social-Media Mistakes."

3. **Putting people down, cursing, or making racist statements.** Do I really have to explain this one? It is rude and unkind, and there can

be consequences. During the London Olympics in 2012, Greek triple jumper Voula Papachristou was kicked off her team for her tweets mocking African immigrants, and Swiss soccer player Michel Morganella was banned from the Olympics for his racist tweet about South Koreans.

4. **Not controlling privacy.** You need to pay attention when posting. Make sure you don't post things publicly when you intend them to be private. A Dutch girl's party invitation went viral after she forgot to use any privacy settings when she asked her friends to her sixteenth birthday party. Over 4,000 people showed up, and 34 people were arrested.

Even private posts don't always stay private. Remember that the people you share with can always share your information with others.

POINT TO PONDER

The Internet does not forget. While talking to students during his first term in the White House, President Obama warned them to "be careful about what you post on Facebook. In the YouTube age, whatever you do, it will be pulled up again later somewhere in your life."

68. The Big Three:
Where Do You Want to Be?

Even your grandmother knows that Facebook, Twitter, and LinkedIn are social-media sites. Although new would-be contenders are popping up every day, these are still the Big Three. And no matter what other sites you patronize for fun and entertainment, make sure you use each one of these three wisely for professional success.

The Big Three are among the first places that current and future clients, customers, coworkers, business colleagues, and potential employers will look you up. Following are some suggestions to ensure that your presence on the Big Three will help, not hurt, your career.

LinkedIn

Thank you. You really encouraged me to join LinkedIn. Within two weeks I had a job offer.

—Feedback from a jury consultant after
an executive coaching session

LinkedIn is the social network for business professionals—a way to connect with people and for people to connect with you.

To participate, simply log on to linkedin.com and set up an account, answering some questions and providing information about your work history. Make sure your profile is 100 percent complete with a professionally appropriate photograph (see Etiquette 71, "Social-Media Guidelines for Photographs"). Include your current contact information, and keep people up-to-date on your accomplishments. Mention your awards and any honors.

When you ask someone to connect with you, personalize your

request. You can add to LinkedIn's basic message by reminding people of your connection. You want quality, not quantity, connections. Nevertheless, strive to have 500 contacts. That's the cut-off number that's posted on your profile, and achieving this goal can give you a certain credibility in your profession.

Make sure you have some recommendations on your site. If people haven't added them independently, you can request them from people who know you and value your work. Thank the person for the recommendation. Remember that it's a two-way street—you should provide recommendations for others who have done good work. LinkedIn recently added an endorsement feature—a quick way to recommend someone's skills and expertise. Again, remember that what goes around, comes around.

Actively participate. Join groups that are suitable for your field, and join groups to which your customers and clients belong. Contribute to the group discussions.

When you receive a LinkedIn update on one of your contacts, send congratulations when appropriate. Politely ask your contacts to introduce you to people in their networks. Make sure you explain why you want to meet a particular person. Use LinkedIn Jobs if you are looking for work.

Twitter

The husband of Yahoo's CEO, Marissa Mayer, announced the birth of their son on Twitter: "Baby boy Bogue born last night. Mom (@marissamayer) and baby are doing great—we couldn't be more excited!"

Twitter allows you to engage with people—those you know and others you don't know—and people to engage with you, in information snippets of 140 characters or less, called *tweets*. Once you open an account on twitter.com, you can attract followers—the people who will receive your tweets—and elect to follow others—whose tweets you will receive. People share their thoughts on everything, including their life, their areas of expertise, current events, politics, any articles they have read, or any topic about which they have opinions.

As I said at the beginning of this etiquette segment: be careful what you tweet. People have gotten fired based on their comments. You don't want to find yourself on Investopedia's list of "Famous Cases of Stupid Tweets That Got People Fired." People also have sent *direct messages* (DMs) thinking they were private messages to specific recipients but instead have sent them to all their followers.

Twitter is being used more and more to communicate news, especially breaking news. According to Twitter, during the 2012 presidential election, people sent 31 million election-related tweets on election night.

Business professionals and organizations also have realized that Twitter is a powerful business tool, and they have gotten on the bandwagon. For example:

- Mayor Jeri Muoio of West Palm Beach, Florida, will answer questions about the government or the future of West Palm Beach on the city's Twitter account, @westpalmbch, with the hashtag #askmuoio. (Using a hashtag with a keyword, such as #businessetiquette, allows people to search for tweets on that topic.)

- Reporters and television newscasters often reference comments made on Twitter about their topics, or they include their subjects' Twitter comments in written articles.

- CEOs are starting to tweet. They appear more accessible when they do. Aetna's CEO Mark Bertolini tweeted the news about his son's kidney transplant, and he also responded to a cancer patient who had tweeted about a problem with his medical coverage. Bertolini agreed to cover the patient's bills, and he tweeted: "The system is broken and I am committed to fixing it."

Facebook

Like most social-media sites, Facebook is easy to join—just log on to facebook.com and follow a few simple steps. It's after you join that you can run into trouble, usually by not being prudent about what you post on your page. Even though Facebook is favored by friends and family to connect with one another, there are business concerns. Consider these five points:

1. **What you post on your personal page can get you fired.** This has been said numerous times, in this book and all over the Internet, yet people still post ridiculous, sometimes horrible things. And those kinds of posts can get you fired. A woman in California was fired from her job (and attracted the attention of the Secret Service) after posting a racial slur about President Obama on her Facebook page after he won a second term.

2. **Your photos and comments create an impression of you.** Do you really want your employer, or possible future employers, seeing photos that depict a drunken or exhibitionist version of you? Do you *really* want to gossip about colleagues and bosses? People have called in sick and then posted photos showing them having a grand time at the beach. What were they thinking!

3. **Make a conscious decision about whom you will friend on your page.** Will your Facebook page include just your friends and family, or will you include coworkers?

4. **Decide on an approach for when you don't want to accept a "friend request" from a business associate.** You don't want to offend people by denying their requests. Think about the person asking to be a friend, and consider what would be the best way to say no without hurting your relationship:

   • You can explain that you are saving Facebook for your family and social friends, and ask the person to please join you on LinkedIn.

- You can ignore the request on Facebook and send a LinkedIn request instead.

- You can accept the invitation and use the privacy controls on your page to limit which sections of your profile the business associate can see.

POINT TO PONDER

Keep in mind that privacy controls are no guarantee that something you post will stay private. Your image, video, or link may be shared by a friend of yours, and then a friend of his, and so on. That's how posts can go viral.

---

5. **Consider whether you should friend your boss.** Though the line between one's personal and professional lives has narrowed (especially true for younger workers who have grown up sharing on social media), think about what you typically post on your sites before you answer the question. Are your posts mostly innocuous comments, or do you sometimes make judgmental comments about your colleagues or company? Do you post photos that show potentially inappropriate behavior? Do you use a lot of language that others might find offensive?

Don't say to yourself, "My boss knows me. My social-media profile doesn't matter." What you post will influence how that person views you professionally, and that could affect your next promotion and your career. If you have any concerns, don't do it. And now, reread numbers 1 and 2 above: if you value your career, you shouldn't be indulging in these kinds of posts anyway.

Other Popular Platforms

Unless marketing a company or product is part of their jobs, most businesspeople will use some of the numerous other social-media sites mostly for personal or recreational reasons.

Among the more popular sites are YouTube, which has been around a very long time and allows you to share videos with others; Instagram, which facilitates photo sharing; Pinterest, a digital scrapbook of photos and images on an endless variety of topics; and Foursquare, a kind of personal GPS, where members note their locations and track their friends via mobile phones and earn rewards for checking in to specific locations and businesses.

Remember, however, that although you may be using these sites for fun, you should always be prepared for someone from your workplace or your professional life to become aware of what you are doing on them.

69. Has Social Media Taken over Your Professional Life?

Birthday cakes are made for people to be together. They give friends a place to gather and celebrate. But too much cake probably isn't healthy. So birthday cake is a lot like Facebook.
—Posted by Facebook on its official page

You can't be on every social-media site and still have time for work and the rest of your life. Even Facebook, as the above quote illustrates, realizes that people can become so involved in social media that they can overdo it. Make sure your social networking doesn't negatively influence your career:

1. **Follow your company guidelines.** Many companies have developed policies about social networking by employees during company time, and they often specify what company information is okay or not okay to share. Some companies even block access to social-media sites completely. Make sure you are familiar with your employer's rules.

2. **Stay productive.** Employees can spend a great deal of time throughout the workday updating or checking their social-media sites. I know when one of my former interns is bored at work, he spends his day tweeting, which is not part of his job. If I know this about him, at some point his employer will surely learn about it too. There are lots of benefits to social networking that have been discussed in this book, but don't let it jeopardize your job. Make sure you attend to your work responsibilities and meet your deadlines.

3. **Don't ignore having in-person visits and making phone calls.** It took four Facebook exchanges with a colleague to determine where and when to meet for lunch. If she had called me, the decision could have been made in seconds. Even my 10-year-old neighbor, who is *so* excited about owning his first smartphone, admits that sometimes it is better to call his friends instead of texting them.

TRY THIS SUGGESTION

Meet with people in person. In an article in the magazine *Fast Company*, author Kevin Purdy explained why he meets weekly with a "semi-regular crew" of guys: "Humans have evolved over many, many years to be very efficient at working with, arguing with, and talking over ideas and pursuits with people, face-to-face. Social-networking tools and remote technology is nowhere near as efficient (yet)."

70. A Blog About Blogs

Do you blog? Should you?

Many of you know that blogs are important marketing tools for businesses. Yet you may not have considered that writing a blog can have positive benefits for you as a businessperson as well. An ebook by Hubspot, *An Introduction to Business Blogging,* states that companies that maintain blogs have 55 percent more website visitors. For you as an individual, having a blog can add to your credibility, improve your writing skills, and provide a creative outlet.

At my suggestion, my son, a recent interior design graduate, started a blog called *How Do You Spell Home?* His comments about space planning, use of accessories, and furniture choices should help to demonstrate to future employers what his interests are in this field and how he implements his ideas.

The following nine suggestions will help you start your own blog:

1. **Just do it.** If you are reading this, then presumably you are already interested in blogs. Go to blogger.com or wordpress.com to set up a free blog. Both those sites, and others, make it very easy to set up your own blog. However, if you work for a company, make sure you are familiar with its policy on blogging before you start tapping away on your keyboard. If it has such a policy, be careful to follow its directives.

2. **Determine your purpose.** Concentrate on a specific area that will allow you to develop, or continue to develop, an area of expertise or interest. Ask yourself: Is there a particular part of my job that I want to explore? Am I a seasoned professional who could help others by sharing my knowledge? Will blogging about my profession cause prospective employers to view me as

a serious candidate? Do I want to share my hobby experiences with others?

3. **Attend to the logistics.** Choose a blog name and design that will keep you focused on your area of interest. Mine is *Pachter's Pointers: Business Etiquette Tips and Career Suggestions*. Put your photo, a short bio, and your contact information on your site. Include a link for people to sign up to receive your blog by email.

4. **Have a schedule.** If you set a time frame (for example, once a week or twice a month) for posting commentary to your blog, you are more apt to keep it up-to-date. Companies may blog daily, but you need to establish a schedule that is realistic for you.

5. **Keep it professional.** Once the blog is posted on the Internet, it's there forever, and you never know who will see it. Do not use your blog to vent about your coworkers, bosses, customers, clients, or anyone else. One teacher lost her job because she talked negatively about her students in her blog. If you are unsure whether you should blog about something, don't!

6. **Use a catchy title for each posting.** Using "how to" or a number in the title can be very successful (the title of Etiquette 76, "Three Tips for Writing Email in Today's Casual Workplace," is a good example). Also, if you include your industry keywords in the title, your blog is more likely to appear when people search those words (the title of Etiquette 65, "The Etiquette of Talking *to* Your Phone," is a good example).

7. **Become a resource.** Add links to other sites that support your comments. Photos or graphics will enhance the text. Tie your comments to current events. Commenting in an informed way on timely issues or concerns can help you become a thought leader in your industry.

8. **Write well.** Writing a blog is a great way to improve your writing skills. Your comments should be clear and concise and easy

for others to read. Keep paragraphs short, but vary their length. Eliminate long, rambling sentences. Use bullets. Edit what you write before you post it, to make sure there are no spelling errors or typos.

9. **Let people know about your blog.** Post your blog to your Twitter, LinkedIn, and Facebook accounts. If possible, include social-media-sharing buttons. Share your blog with your groups on LinkedIn. Add your blog address to your personal email signature. Put your blog address on your résumé and business card. Find other sites that will post your blog. For example, Blogher .com, the largest community of women who blog, has posted my blogs on its site.

These suggestions should help you get started. But to hone your skills, continue to read some of the many articles that have been written about successful blogging.

71. Social-Media Guidelines
for Photographs

I looked up a potential vendor on LinkedIn. When she showed up in person at a meeting, I had no idea who she was. She looked nothing like her LinkedIn photo.   —Senior manager at an educational company

Your image is conveyed through your photograph, and it's part of the first impression you make on others. What are you conveying? Many businesspeople have posted photographs of themselves on LinkedIn and other sites that detract from their professionalism.

Post a professionally appropriate photograph. You want to look like a credible, approachable person, not like you just came from the beach.

It is important to include a photograph when it's possible to do so. It can also help in making sure that people know that they have connected with the right person. There could be many "Thomas Millers."

Use the following seven guidelines for posting photographs of yourself on social media:

1. **Post a headshot.** This type of photograph highlights your head and face but often shows your shoulders and part of your chest. You are the focus of the picture.

2. **Choose a recent photo that flatters you.** Sounds obvious, but people don't always pay attention to their choice. This does not mean a glamour shot, but you should look like a competent professional in the photograph. If your photo is more than 8 to 10 years old, people may be very surprised when they meet you.

3. **Appear in front of a clear, uncluttered background that is well lit.** There shouldn't be any dark shadows obscuring your face. People must be able to see you clearly.

4. **Make sure your face is in focus.** The background can be slightly out of focus, but your features need to be sharp, not blurred.

5. **Wear appropriate professional or business casual attire.** Appear as you usually would in a business situation. This may also mean that you are freshly shaven or wearing makeup and jewelry.

6. **Look at the camera and keep your head straight.** Women have a tendency to tilt their heads, and they look less self-assured when they do. Have a pleasant facial expression. If you are frowning or scowling, why would someone want to hire or work with you?

7. **Be cautious with an environmental portrait.** This type of photo places you in a setting that relates to your profession. This is generally a wider shot, and your face is a smaller part of the photograph. These pictures are often used as additional photos on a website, and are not recommended for headshot postings.

TRY THIS SUGGESTION

Hire a professional photographer. If the above guidelines seem overwhelming, hire someone who takes photos for a living. It's worth the investment.

72. Almost as Good as the Real Thing: Skype

I was amazed at how effective the discussion was via Skype.
The only thing we weren't able to do was shake hands!

That's what I told a reporter from the *Cleveland Plain Dealer* when she asked me about using Skype for a one-on-one, long-distance coaching session. And I meant it. Skype is an excellent and inexpensive alternative if you are not able to meet with a client in person.

Today, companies often prescreen candidates on Skype before bringing potential employees into the main office for an in person meeting. Others use Skype to connect remotely with colleagues in different locations. And many coaches can now work with individuals around the world because of Skype. From my office in New Jersey, I have worked with professionals who are located all over the United States. I even had a discussion about coaching with a woman in Uganda.

Here are seven suggestions to help you to communicate effectively using Skype:

1. **Test the equipment before a meeting or interview.** Make sure your Skype connection is working properly. Five minutes before the start of a meeting is not the time to find out that you do not have any volume.

2. **Use a nondistracting background that is clear and uncluttered.** Make sure your location has good lighting. Be careful if you have a window behind you. If it is bright outside, you will appear as a dark silhouette. Run a test with a friend or colleague to make sure you look good in your surroundings.

3. **Practice.** Remember you are creating a snapshot of yourself. Practice so that you know how you come across. People tend to overgesture. This behavior is distracting when you are on Skype.

4. **Make sure your clothing is appropriate**. Just because you are not meeting in person does not mean the interviewer or business associate cannot see what you are wearing. And don't assume only your upper body is showing. Dress professionally from head to toe.

5. **Smile.** Let your personality shine through. Speak audibly and clearly. Talk to the camera—keep in mind that when you are looking at your computer screen, you may appear to be looking down; when you look directly at the camera, you will appear to be looking your Skype partner in the eye. And just as in any interview, be prepared for the questions.

6. **Control interruptions.** Make sure in advance that there will be no phones ringing and no people walking in and out of your room.

7. **Don't stay on too long.** Remember that meetings on Skype shouldn't go as long as face-to-face meetings. Being on camera can be exhausting for many people.

73. Email Etiquette 1: Avoid Saying or Doing the Wrong Thing

Email remains one of the most important ways in which people communicate in today's workplace, yet businesspeople still make embarrassing mistakes when sending messages to customers, colleagues, bosses, or potential employers.

Follow these suggestions to avoid errors and to make sure your emails convey a professional message:

1. **Double-check that you have selected the correct recipient.** Pay attention when typing a name from your address book on the email's "To" line. It is easy to select the wrong name, which can be embarrassing to you and to the person who receives the email by mistake.

2. **Add the email address last.** You don't want to send an email accidentally before you have finished writing and proofing the message. Even when you are replying to a message, it's a good precaution to delete the recipient's address and insert it only when you are sure the message is ready to be sent.

3. **Choose a good subject line.** People often decide whether to open an email based on the subject line. Choose one that lets readers know you are addressing their concerns or business issues. Examples include:

   • Quick question about your presentation

   • Amber Jones suggested that I contact you [assuming both people know Amber]

   • Suggestions for the proposal

4. **Do not come across as sounding abrupt**. Read your message out loud. If it sounds harsh to you, it will sound harsh to the reader. Avoid negative words such as *failure*, *wrong*, or *neglected*. Use *please* and *thank you*.

5. **Use a salutation and a closing**. You'll seem friendlier if you do. Starting your email with "Hi Mark," "Hello Sally," or "Dear Juan" sets a pleasant tone. End your message with a closing: "Thanks," "Regards," or "Best," followed by your name.

6. **Make your message easy to read.** Looks count. Vary the length of your sentences and paragraphs. Long sentences or paragraphs are more difficult to read, especially on the computer screen. Use bullets to set off points you want to make.

7. **Be cautious with humor.** Something perceived as funny when spoken may come across very differently when written. When in doubt, leave it out.

8. **Think twice before hitting "Reply all."** Make sure that everyone on the list needs to receive the email. People complain often that they receive email messages that they just don't need to see.

9. **Use a signature block.** Include your phone number and a physical address where someone can contact you directly. You also may want to include your social-media information. Be cautious about using quotations under your signature. Remember, this is business.

10. **Proofread every message.** Mistakes will be noticed, and depending upon the recipient, you may be judged for making them. Spell-checkers do not replace your good brain. One supervisor intended to write "Sorry for the inconvenience." But he relied on his spell-checker and ended up writing "Sorry for the incontinence."

POINT TO PONDER

Use a professional email address. If you work for a company, you will use your company email address. But if you are not employed currently or you occasionally use your personal email for work-related items, be careful when choosing a personal email address. "Hotmama@ . . ." or "Diva@ . . ." or "thesexyone@ . . ." are not appropriate addresses for use in the workplace. Also make sure your address conveys your name, so the recipient knows who sent the email—for example, Tom.Smith@gmail.com or TSmith@ xyz.com. Otherwise, your message may go straight to the "Delete" file.

74. Email Etiquette 2:
Still Puzzling After All These Years

Though email has been around for a while, I still get numerous questions from businesspeople and reporters about how to use it appropriately in the business world. Here are some of the more recent questions:

Q. *I see both e-mail and email. What is the correct spelling?*
A. Both are correct, as long as you consistently spell the word the same way throughout a document. But remember that our language is always evolving. When the *AP Stylebook* was revised recently, the hyphen disappeared from *email* within its covers. Most print media in the United States follow the Associated Press (AP) style. I too have eliminated the hyphen in *email*.

Q. *I received an email that clearly wasn't intended for me. Should I let the sender know?*
A. If the sender will be expecting a reply, you need to let that person know. One woman in a similar situation wrote: "I know you're very busy, but I don't think you meant to send this email to me. And I wanted to let you know so you can send it to the correct person."

Q. *I need to send an email to a group of people. What would be an appropriate salutation? I have used, "Hi all," but that sounds awkward.*
A. You could use "Hello Everyone." You could also just say "Hello."

Q. *I send a lot of emails to people I have not met. I always begin addressing the emails to a Ms. or Mr. "last name." If, after corresponding through several emails, the person signs all of his or her responses with just a first name, can I start addressing my emails to the first name?*

A. The general guideline about switching to first names is, as you stated, when a person signs his or her first name. This is your signal to respond using the first name. If you don't, you may appear stiff and impersonal.

Q. *I never know at what point I no longer need to respond to someone's emails. Any suggestions?*
A. If the person needs to know that you received the information, or the person has helped you, you need to respond. A quick "Thanks" is usually all that is needed.

Q. *What color ink and font sizes are acceptable in business emails?*
A. With all the options available on computers, it can be tempting to get carried away, using large fonts or very small fonts, and different colors. Don't. Make your emails easy for others to read. Black ink is appropriate for all business writing—including emails. Generally, it is best to use 10- or 12-point type and an easy-to-read font such as Arial, Calibri, or Times New Roman.

Q. *I just encountered at work the "danger" of writing an email directly to one person without considering the fact that the email may be forwarded or shared with others. I was embarrassed. Was it okay for the recipient to forward my email?*
A. A basic guideline is to assume that others will see what you write, so don't write anything you wouldn't want everyone to see. Email is easy for people to forward to others. Ideally, people would forward only good news and general information, but that doesn't always happen. Better safe than sorry.

ONE MORE TIME: EMAIL LEAVES A TRAIL

No matter how many times people hear the message, it just doesn't seem to get through. Don't put *anything* into email that you wouldn't be comfortable sharing with the world. Because if the (former) head of the CIA can get caught in 2012, so can you.

In a now infamous scandal, the affair between CIA chief General David Petraeus and his female biographer came to light because of her supposedly anonymous emails warning off another woman. The resulting investigation brought to light revealing email exchanges between the general and his biographer—even though the duo apparently thought they were avoiding detection by using email drafts on a shared account, instead of using email messages via a regular account, to communicate.

The lesson for the rest of us? *Every* electronic communication leaves a trail. As I told a reporter from *NBC News* at the time: what you say, or write, can come back to haunt you. And all too often, it does.

75. Are You Putting Yourself Down as You Write?

During a writing class for a corporation's new hires, most of them recent college graduates, a number of the participants used self-discounting language when they communicated with their colleagues as well as with those higher up the corporate ladder. The self-discounting terms they used included *kinda, just, actually, perhaps, I wonder,* and *I hope.*

For example, when they wanted to set up a meeting with someone, some of them wrote in this manner: "I was just wondering if you perhaps had some time to meet with me." Or when they submitted information: "I have enclosed the sample. I hope it is sufficient."

When I asked them why they expressed themselves this way, they said that they didn't want to come across as pushy. My comment was that by trying not to be pushy, they were coming across as passive, tentative, and too deferential for the business world.

I suggested an alternative approach, a middle ground that I call *polite and powerful.* They could use words that are polite but that would not diminish them. Among the suggestions were these:

- **Eliminate self-discounting words.** Instead of saying, "I actually got the promotion," say, "I got the promotion."

- **Use a question.** Instead of saying something like, "I was just wondering if you perhaps had some time to meet with me," use the straightforward query: "Would you have some time this week to meet with me?"

- **Be direct.** Instead of "I hope it is sufficient," say, "If you need additional information, just let me know."

TRY THIS SUGGESTION

Monitor your outgoing emails over the next couple of weeks, and start eliminating your self-discounting language. You may be surprised at how much of it you find.

76. Three Tips for Writing Email in Today's Casual Workplace

Oh, man. That's disappointing for us.

Since she knows I teach business writing, a colleague asked my opinion about the above sentence, which was part of an email she received from a potential client. She found the use of "Oh, man" very amusing.

My response was that "Oh, man" is very casual language that conveys the impression that the sentence was written by a young person. My son often used that phrase as a teenager, when he was upset.

How you write is part of your professional image. Your word choice conveys a lot about you. Though the business world is more informal today than in the past, there are some overly casual expressions and forms of punctuation that you should avoid when writing emails so you don't undermine your professionalism. Among them are these:

- **Referring to people as *you guys* or *folks*.** These are laid-back, colloquial expressions and should be avoided when writing or speaking in the business world. For example, never say, "Is there any way *you guys* can help me out?" (Simply say *you*.) Nor should you say, "The *folks* from marketing were here this morning." (Use *group*, *coworkers*, *team*, or *people* instead of *folks*.)

- **Using *Hey* or *Yo* as a salutation.** The relaxed nature of our writings should not affect the salutation in an email. *Hey* is a very informal salutation ("Hey, Colby"), and generally it should not be used in the workplace. And *Yo* is not okay either. Use *Hi* or *Hello* instead.

    Also, do not shorten someone's name. Use the person's full name ("Hi, Michael") unless you know it is okay to call him "Mike."

- **Overusing the exclamation point.** People sometimes get carried away and put a number of exclamation points at the end of their sentences. The result can appear too emotional or immature. Exclamation points should be used sparingly in writing. If you must use an exclamation point, use only one. I'll never forget the email I received that said: "The meeting is Monday. Everyone must attend!!!!!!!!!!"

INSTANT MESSAGING SUGGESTIONS

Instant messaging (IM) is a quick and easy way to connect with your colleagues in real time. It's similar to stopping briefly at someone's office to gain information or answers to your questions—but without leaving your desk. The speed and ease of instant messaging may be why I am rarely asked questions about this type of communication. Even so, here are some points to remember:

1. **Use a short greeting.** All you need to write is "Hi" or "Hi Bill." Check to make sure it is a good time to chat.
2. **Keep your comments brief.** If your comments or discussion will be lengthy, generally you want to use email or call the person rather than using instant messaging.
3. **Give the person your undivided attention.** It's easy to miss things if you don't.
4. **IM messages can be saved.** Be careful what you say, just as you should in an email.

77. Doing the Write Thing: Always Look for One

I had coffee with a colleague at a very nice cafe in New York. After we paid the bill, the waiter gave us a postcard with the restaurant's information on it. Unfortunately, the restaurant's name was misspelled in the Internet address.

It is unprofessional and potentially costly to an organization to have mistakes in its promotional materials or other documents.

In my writing classes, I teach the *always-look-for-one concept*. This means that when you are proofing your writings, keep looking until you find an error. And if you don't find one, keep looking until you do, or until you are absolutely sure your work is error-free. It is easy to miss errors unless you have a strategy for finding them.

When we mentioned to the waiter that we had noticed a mistake in the postcard, he responded that the cafe's owner had found the error when the cards came back from the printer. He still wanted waiters to give out the cards, however, hoping that customers would recognize and correct the mistake.

Following the always-look-for-one rule *before* the cards were printed would have been a better alternative.

Additional proofreading tips include these:

- **Read your message out loud syl-la-ble by syl-la-ble.** If you read the words slowly, you will often hear any mistakes.

- **Have someone else proof your writing.** It is easier for other people to catch your mistakes because they read what you've written with fresh eyes.

- **Double-check your numbers.** Make sure you have the commas and periods in the right places. It can be very costly—literally—if you make a mistake. A man wrote that he had paid "$20000" for his software program. Did he mean to say "$20,000" or "$200.00"?

DID YOU CATCH THE ERROR?

The following sentence was included in a recent email advertising a writing seminar:

> *Don't spend another day struggling to write business documents with that are on target, on topic, and on deadline.*

Can you find a mistake in the sentence? Would a gaffe affect your decision to sign up for the class? It would certainly discourage some potential attendees. It is unprofessional and potentially costly to have mistakes in your documents.

PS: The error in the sentence? The word "with" should have been deleted.

78. Writing for an International Audience?
Vive la difference!

During one of my presentation skills classes, an international participant said he had received an email telling him to meet his colleagues in the parking lot at 5 p.m. on the dot. He told the class, "I arrived on time, but I kept looking, and I couldn't find the dot!"

The above illustration highlights one of my suggestions for anyone who is writing for an international audience: avoid the use of buzzwords, jargon, or colloquialisms. Even for those who are fluent in English, some of our expressions can be confusing, or even strange—consider the statement "It's raining cats and dogs."

Other suggestions include these:

- **Use the correct salutation.** Generally, it is best to use last names with the appropriate honorific ("Dear Mr. Schmidt"). It's more respectful when you do, and internationally that can be very important. Don't use first names, nicknames, or the diminutive form of someone's name ("Bob" for "Robert," for instance, or "Trish" for "Patricia") unless you know it is okay to do so.

- **Spell out all dates.** In the United States, "2/3/13" is the shortened form for February 3, 2013. In other countries, such as Australia, where the first numeral denotes the day, it means March 2, 2013.

- **Understand how cultural differences can influence writing.** High-context cultures (Japanese, Arab, or Chinese) want to get to know you, and people from these cultures can be very personal in their writings. I received a letter from a potential client in Malaysia that began, "Hello Dear Barbara," yet I had met the man only once.

Low-context cultures (German, American, or Scandinavian) are more straightforward, and people from these cultures can get to the point very quickly.

- **Know the differences between American and British English.** An Australian publication used one of my press releases about holiday travel, but it rewrote the release using British English. For example:

  - Keeping your cool during the holidays can be a challenge, especially since passengers are paying more and still enduring long lines, cancellations, delays, and lost luggage [the U.S. sentence].

  - Travelling during the holidays can be mega-stressful with long queues, dodgy weather in some destinations, and hordes of people [the Australian version].

  Did you notice the following:

  - **Different words.** The British word for *line* is *queue*. Also *dodgy* is not commonly used in America to mean *unreliable*. And in many British countries, the word *holidays* refers not only to special days but also to what Americans call *vacations*.

  - **Spelling differences.** The Australian version used the British spelling of *travelling*. The U.S. spelling is *traveling*. Some other examples of American and British spelling differences include *color* and *colour*, *check* and *cheque*, and *theater* and *theatre*.

═SECTION IV═
CAREER

Because the dynamics of the workplace are continually evolving, there are always more skills to be learned by anyone who takes an active, enthusiastic role in his or her own career development—and, since you are reading this book, that includes you.

These are the skills that will give you a competitive edge in your career. They will give you the poise and self-assurance that enable you to advance in your career and have others see you as someone interested in that advancement.

The articles in this last section address how to become a valuable employee, look for a job, give an effective presentation, and be assertive in the workplace and your life. Individually they are important, but collectively, they will help you to create the skill set and adaptability you need to take you to the next level in your career.

79. The Workers' Seven Deadly Sins Can Kill Your Career

A colleague told me that she had had to fire one of her employees because he hadn't shown any initiative in her fast-paced, creative work environment.

I thought about this for a moment and responded that he had committed one of the *Workers' Seven Deadly Sins*—the career-killing work traits that get employees ignored, not promoted, or even fired.

In today's workplace, it's not enough simply to perform your job at an acceptable level—you want to be seen as a valuable and vital employee. You want to become someone with whom others want to work. Ask yourself if you exhibit any of the boldface traits below, and resolve to eliminate them if you do:

1. **Not showing initiative.** Are you trying new or better ways to accomplish your work? Is your employer gaining anything extra from you? As my colleague's employee found out, most employers want you to go above and beyond the basic requirements.

2. **Not paying attention to details.** Are there mistakes in your work? Do you notice the little things, proofread your writings, and double-check any numbers? There can be consequences if you don't. One engineer wrote the wrong house number on a work order, and his employees ripped up the wrong driveway.

3. **Not offering to help**. You need to do your own work, but you also, whenever possible, need to offer to help others. You come across as a team player when you do—somebody others want to work with. Plus, you may learn new skills and meet new people. Added benefits!

4. **Not staying current with changes in your profession.** You don't want to be left behind. Stay abreast of any trends in your field. Continue learning. Take advantage of any training your company offers. Stay up-to-date with technology, including social media.

5. **Not connecting with others.** This has been discussed in other parts of the book, but it bears repeating. People don't like to work with colleagues who ignore them. Smile. Be friendly. Make an effort to say "Hello," "Good morning," and so on, not only to people you know but also to those you don't know.

6. **Not conveying enthusiasm for your job.** Show interest in your work. Be eager to get the job done. Arrive on time, or early. Stay late when necessary. Give sincere compliments. Speak well of others, avoid downbeat topics, and stop complaining. Don't criticize your employer, boss, or coworkers on your social-media sites.

POINT TO PONDER

During a lunch break, a number of employees were complaining about their jobs. One woman at the table interrupted them and said: "I love having a job in today's economy. And that's enough to make me enthusiastic about my work." What a great attitude.

7. **Not having a professional demeanor.** You want to convey a confident and credible image. Be aware of your verbal and nonverbal communication. Are you speaking too softly or loudly? Are you dressing appropriately for your position? Do you use filler words (*okay, all right, like*) that detract from your comments?

80. How Open Are You to Feedback?

Not long ago, I received a note from a vendor after giving him some critical feedback about a business transaction I had with his company. He wrote:

> *I take a lot of pride in my work and in my business, and even though it is difficult to hear negative comments upon completion of a job, I respect and appreciate your honesty. Your feedback will go a long way in helping me grow my business.*

What a great response to my comments. Would you respond in a similar manner if you heard criticism about your work?

It is easy to brush feedback aside or to make excuses. Yet, you can gain valuable insights from the comments of others. As a speaker, I receive feedback from seminar participants all the time. I love hearing the many wonderful comments, but I also truly appreciate the suggestions for improvement—many of which have been implemented in my classes.

The next time you receive feedback, review your response against this list. Did you react in any of the following ways:

1. **Get defensive?** Don't shut down. You want to be open to feedback. Look at the person making the comments. Don't frown or cross your arms. Remember, no one is perfect. We all make mistakes. Think of criticism as an opportunity to grow.

2. **Listen to the person?** Let the individual complete his or her thoughts. And, hard as it may be, do not interrupt or argue. You really need to hear what the person has to say.

3. **Ask yourself: Who is giving you the feedback?** If the feedback is from a customer, you need to consider the suggestions and implement them, if appropriate. If the feedback is from your boss, generally it's advisable to make the suggested changes.

4. **Learn as much as you could?** If the person is not specific, you can ask him or her to explain the comments. Responses like "What exactly do you mean by 'unprofessional'?" or "Why did you say the report was terrible?" not only help you gain information but also buy you some time to calm down, if necessary, and collect your thoughts. You could also add "Tell me more," which lets the person know you are open to feedback.

5. **Engage in the discussion?** Paraphrase what you have heard. Saying something like "You're suggesting that . . ." will ensure that you have grasped the person's points. You also may want to explain, without making an excuse. For example, people occasionally will correct what they believe is an error in something I have written. If I am sure that I am correct, I will respond, politely, that their comments reflect only one way of writing. Rules may differ depending upon the style manual used, and we are most likely using different manuals.

6. **Acknowledge or fix the problem?** Sometimes you can acknowledge the mistake by saying, "You're right. It won't happen again." This usually ends the discussion. In other situations, you may want to let the person know what you will be doing differently in the future. This can be done on the spot or at a later time. One woman wrote to her client: "Thanks for the feedback. I have already implemented the changes we discussed, and I look forward to working with you in the future."

7. **Thank the person?** Receiving feedback is an opportunity to improve your skills or your business and to maintain your relationship with the person. Whether your critic's comments are positive or negative, at the end of the conversation, make sure you say "Thank you" or "Thanks for sharing your thoughts. I appreciate it."

POINT TO PONDER

Do you perceive a pattern in the feedback you get about your work? A solitary criticism or observation may be just one person's opinion, but if you notice a lot of similar comments, chances are there is some truth to the feedback—positive or negative.

81. Don't Put Yourself Down: Accept Compliments

While teaching a class on presentations skills, I complimented a woman on how much improvement she had made over the course of the day.

She replied, "Not really. I still have a lot more to improve upon."

Her comment got me thinking about how quickly we negate compliments. It is so easy for people to deflect the nice things others say about them.

Yes, my participant still had more to learn, but she also needed to acknowledge how much she had accomplished. When you concentrate only on the negative, it's hard to be motivated to continue learning. When you focus on what you have achieved, you are more likely to embrace a positive approach to future growth.

Both men and women negate compliments:

- A man responded to my compliment that he had nice handwriting by saying, "Oh, it's my pen!"

- A sales representative responded to her manager, after he had commented on her excellent sales numbers, "Oh, I don't know how that happened. It must have been a fluke."

If someone pays you a compliment, don't discount it. Simply say "Thank you." If you feel comfortable doing so, you can add more. Examples include: "Thank you. I appreciate that." Or "Thank you. I appreciate your comments." Or "Thank you. I worked hard on that assignment. Your words mean a lot to me."

82. Toot Your Own Horn

The woman was well educated, well groomed, and spoke like a professional. Yet when asked about herself, she did not speak of her accomplishments, and she was very self-deprecating. When asked why, she responded, "I don't want to sound like I'm bragging."

Many people don't talk about or post their accomplishments, or they discount themselves and their achievements with statements like "Oh, what I did was no big deal."

In the business world, you can limit your chances of success when others don't know what you do or what you have accomplished. Skillful self-promotion is a business strength. You don't want to sound like a braggart, but you do want to toot your own horn when appropriate.

Here are six suggestions for promoting yourself successfully:

1. **Be visible**. Get involved at your company. Join any company clubs or activities that interest you. Use the work gym, if there is one. Volunteer for assignments. Offer to make presentations, and volunteer to train others. If possible, write articles for your company publications. Run for office in your professional and community organizations.

2. **Enter competitions and apply for awards**. A lot of people avoid doing this—they say it's too self-serving. Yet, winning awards is a way for people who know you, but especially those who *don't* know you, to find out about your talents. It builds your credibility. And make sure you promote your successes. For instance, my selection as one of the Best 50 Women in Business in New Jersey by *NJBIZ Magazine* is highlighted in my email signature block.

3. **Post your accomplishments on your social-media sites (LinkedIn, Face-book, Twitter, and the like).** However, be careful not to mention the same accomplishment over and over. You can overdo it and make yourself sound like a braggart. There is a balance. You must speak of other things, not just about what you do well.

4. **Have a prepared self-introduction.** You may find yourself in situations in which you have to introduce yourself. Being prepared will allow you to be comfortable speaking about yourself. Make sure you say your full name and add a few brief comments about yourself.

5. **When asked, do tell.** If someone asks you how you are doing at work, it is your opportunity to mention your accomplishments. Without going into too much detail, tell the person about any recent promotions, new projects, additional responsibilities, and so on.

TRY THIS SUGGESTION

Speak well of others. You appear gracious when you speak of other peoples' accomplishments, not just your own.

6. **Weave your accomplishments into conversation, when appropriate.** For example, when I talk in seminars about how men tend to interrupt more than women during meetings, I mention comments from my seminar participants in Oman, in the Middle East. These remarks add to the discussion, and they also highlight my international experience.

83. The Importance of Role Models, Mentors, and Networks

A member of my network asked me to meet with one of his students. I was glad to help him, as he had helped me in the past. The young woman was a recent graduate and needed career advice. Since she was just entering the workplace, we spent a lot of time discussing the importance of role models, mentors, and networks.

Do you have a role model, mentor, or network? Employees who move up in organizations often have these resources in common. These workers know it is important to have people they can count on, and from whom they can learn.

Role Models

A role model can be someone you know or someone you don't know, but either way, this person doesn't take an active role in your career development. A role model is a person who inspires you because he or she proves that it is possible to achieve your dreams.

A role model is someone you learn from simply by watching his or her behavior, listening to what he or she has to say, or reading about his or her life and accomplishments. Don't be envious of the accomplishments of others. Instead, let them inspire you to do great things.

POINT TO PONDER

Dr. Mae Jemison, the first black woman to travel in space, credits the fictional Lieutenant Uhura on the television show *Star Trek* as her inspiration for becoming an astronaut.

Mentors

A mentor, unlike a role model, is someone who takes an active role in your career development. Mentors often provide specific career advice for you. A mentor can make a tremendous difference in your career success.

You can have numerous mentors throughout your career. My first mentor helped me to learn photography when very few women were in the profession. Without his input, I never would have become the first woman photographer at one of the 10 largest newspapers in the country. Another mentor was a senior executive at an aerospace company. She helped me learn about the corporate world.

Some organizations have formal mentoring programs for employees. If such a program is available to you, I suggest you sign up. There is also an informal method. In this option, you choose somebody whose work you admire and from whom you think you can learn. Ask that person for advice, and let the relationship naturally develop over time.

Professional Networks

A professional network is a group of professionals who help and support each other. A professional network can be your best friend if you're job hunting or trying to navigate through corporate politics. It's also a great way to interact with experts in your field, though a network doesn't necessarily have to be made up of people who are all in the same profession.

Join your professional associations, and get involved. Most have local chapters. They are excellent places to meet people with more career experience and knowledge in your field. One organization for professional speakers is the National Speakers Association (NSA). I still attend some of the local chapter meetings, as there is always something new to learn.

There are also numerous networks and groups for professionals on social-media sites such as LinkedIn. You can join these and learn from others in your field.

POINT TO PONDER

One recent graduate played golf at his professional association's annual golf outing, and the next day a member of his foursome asked for his résumé.

84. Become a Mentor:
It's a Two-Way Street!

A woman that I have mentored for a number of years called me recently and asked me to help her prepare for a high-level interview. She is being considered for a position as a vice president at another company. She said that a woman she had mentored at that company had recommended her for the open position.

The anecdote made my day! As the old saying observes, what goes around, comes around.

Mentoring is a two-way street. The mentee gains from interacting with an experienced person, but the mentor also benefits from the relationship. Mentors gain by doing the following:

1. **Helping others develop in their careers.** This is the primary role of mentoring. Many people really enjoy helping others, just for the satisfaction of doing so.

2. **Expanding the mentor's professional network.** As the woman I just mentioned experienced, having people you've helped in your network can be very helpful for your own career advancement. As your mentees grow and develop in their fields, they may know people who can help you, or they may know of opportunities that would be good for you.

3. **Learning from the mentee.** You can obtain new perspectives on current issues. Our college interns were invaluable in helping us learn about social media. I always try to mentor a couple of people at any given time. I learn so much from their work experiences.

4. **Strengthening the mentor's role as an expert in his or her field.** You will be sharing your expertise with others, and thereby enhancing your own reputation.

5. **Expanding the mentor's own skills.** When you interact with a mentee, you often need to coach and provide feedback to that person. These are good leadership skills for you to have, regardless of your profession.

6. **Becoming people that others want to work for.** A corporate attorney for a large company had a reputation for developing the people who worked for him. As a result, he always had a large pool of potential hires when he had an open position.

There are many ways to become a mentor. Your company or professional associations may have formal mentoring programs that need mentors. Community organizations also may have programs.

There is also an informal method. In this option, you develop mentoring relationships with people by offering to help them, answering their questions, and inviting them to interact with you. Over time mentoring relationships can develop.

Isn't it time for you to start mentoring others?

85. Internship Tips for My Son . . . and Others

When my son finished his first year at his university, he sought his first internship. Networking helped get him in the door, but he handled himself beautifully during the interview and won the position on his own merits.

Of course, I wanted to give him some advice before he started working, and since he sometimes "hears" me better in writing, I emailed my suggestions to him. These tips would be equally helpful for other first-time interns—or anyone who was starting a new position.

Dear Jacob,

Here are some suggestions to help you shine as an intern:

1. **Know how lucky you are.** Many young people today are not able to find jobs, let alone an internship with a great company. Being able to put an internship on your résumé adds valuable work experience to your qualifications.
2. **Arrive on time, . . . even a little early.** And don't rush out the door at the end of the day. Stay late when you can. Ask your boss before you leave: "Is there anything else I can do before I head out?"
3. **Work hard and do your best.** I know you're not in school and you are not getting graded, but believe me, your work will be evaluated. Meet your deadlines and volunteer for additional assignments.
4. **Listen and observe others.** You are being given a wonderful opportunity to experience the corporate world. Learn all you can.
5. **Don't be shy.** It can seem daunting to be surrounded by professionals, not students. But you don't want to appear intimidated. You want to be viewed as a pleasant, approachable person.

6. **Ask questions when you don't understand.** But try to solve the problem yourself when you can. You don't want to ask a question that you could have answered yourself.

7. **Dress to suit the job.** I already went shopping for you, so this should be easy! Remember you are not going to class. You are going into a business setting. It's usually appropriate to copy the dress style of other employees.

Have a great experience. I am very proud of you.
Love, Mom

PS: I know you know this, but remember: don't put anything inappropriate about your employer on your Facebook page or any other social-networking site.

86. Moving On?
The Etiquette for Leaving a Job

A woman I mentored was leaving her company and wanted some suggestions on how to exit graciously.

Moving to a new position is not unusual in today's workplace. A study by MetLife found that more than one-third of employees hoped to change jobs within 12 months.

My mentee and I discussed four key actions she needed to take, which also apply to anyone facing a similar situation:

1. **Let people know.** Obviously your boss knows, but you need to tell or email your employees, colleagues, clients, and customers. The woman I mentored used the email below to tell a group of her clients at the same company. It could be adapted to fit a variety of situations:

Hello,

    I wanted to reach out to everyone to share some news. This Friday will be my last day.

    Over the past year, you have provided me with the opportunity to grow, you have challenged and supported me, and you've helped me to become a better account supervisor. I am grateful, and I couldn't leave without expressing my appreciation for your many kindnesses.

    I have enjoyed working with all of you. Although I am sad to leave, I will be moving on to a new opportunity to continue my growth and career development.

    I hope to have a chance to see everyone to say goodbye in person.

    All the best,

---

2. **Thank people.** Make a special effort to thank the people who have gone out of their way for you. One departing employee took his office manager to lunch as a special thank you.

3. **Don't burn your bridges.** No matter how long you have fantasized about telling your boss off—don't do it. It might make you feel wonderful for 10 seconds, but later you probably would feel bad about it. And the only thing you would accomplish would be to lose a reference. Also, do not post any nasty or gloating comments on Facebook.

4. **Make the transition easy for your replacement.** Be as up-to-date as you can. Leave detailed notes. If possible, introduce the person replacing you to the key people with whom he or she will be working.

These suggestions worked for my mentee. The last thing her boss said to her was, "You are welcome to come back any time!"

87. Just Do It! Job-Hunting Tips

There are no jobs out there, so why bother looking?

You shouldn't let a discouraging job market stop you from searching for work. Times may be tough, but that means job seekers need to be even more diligent. There are still jobs available, and the professionals who are persistent, prepared, and polished will have an advantage.

Here are 10 tips that may help you land a job:

1. **Approach your job search as if it were your job.** Work every day at your search. Stay focused. Each week, set a number of contacts or connections to make and activities to carry out. It is easy to avoid looking, but if you do that, you won't find a job. If you keep looking, you will increase your chances of finding the right position for you.

2. **Prepare for the search.** Have an up-to-date résumé—or résumés, if you need to tailor your experience to target different kinds of companies. Keep a log of what you have done, the people you have met, and any follow-up actions you need to take. Practice interviewing with a friend, and record yourself on video. You may be surprised by what you see.

3. **Continue to develop yourself.** Take a class, learn a second language, or develop or expand a hobby. These experiences can lead to meeting new people and finding new opportunities. You also can start a blog, writing on different aspects of your profession. What a great way to maintain involvement in your field! (See Etiquette 70, "A Blog About Blogs.")

4. **Check that your online presence won't embarrass you.** Google yourself to find out what future employers will see if they do a search of your name. Many prospective employers will review your social-media sites. Remove any photos showing drunken revelers, foul language, or disparaging remarks about former employers—in fact, remove anything questionable. I know that this could limit your Facebook profile, but the only alternative is to hide your page's content, which might make a recruiter wonder what you are hiding.

POINT TO PONDER

According to a 2012 CareerBuilder study, 37 percent of the nation's employers are using social-networking sites such as LinkedIn, Facebook, and Twitter to screen potential candidates.

5. **Review and use numerous job sites.** In addition to the comprehensive search engines like Indeed.com, look at specific openings on company websites and your professional and alumni associations' job postings. And both LinkedIn and Twitter have job search components on their sites that have helped people find jobs.

6. **Use a multipronged approach.** In addition to using social media, people still find jobs through the want ads in their local paper. Job fairs can be gold mines too. Don't forget to tap into the career center at your alma mater—these centers often have great connections. Let your personal and professional networks know you are looking (see the "Try This Suggestion" box). Also volunteer in your community. Not only will you be helping others but you will also be meeting new people, and you never know whom you might meet or what you may discover—maybe a whole new career passion.

7. **Be open to all options.** If part-time or temporary positions are available, consider taking them. They can provide good experience, and sometimes they can lead to full-time work. Be open to a career change. If an opportunity in a different profession or industry becomes available, think about taking it.

8. **Be cautious with unusual tactics**. Some people have tried walking the streets wearing sandwich boards to advertise their job search, and others have worn t-shirts announcing that they are looking for work. These different approaches sometimes work, but they can just as easily backfire by making you appear unprofessional.

9. **Help others**. What goes around really does come around—so help others whenever you can. Be a resource. If you hear of an opening that is appropriate for someone, let that person know.

10. **Keep your outlook upbeat**. Looking for a job is a stressful experience even in the best of economic times. Eat right, exercise, and get adequate sleep. Don't let negative self-talk take over. Remind yourself that you will find a job. It may take a while in today's economy, but it will happen.

TRY THIS SUGGESTION

A key source of job leads that people often overlook is letting friends, acquaintances, and trusted colleagues know that they are looking for work. You never know what may develop. The following two examples illustrate how beneficial this approach can be—but be careful whom you tell if you don't want your current boss to know:

- A neighbor's friend is a chef. The restaurant where she had worked for years recently closed unexpectedly. When she found herself unemployed, she told her friends and colleagues that she was seeking another position. A colleague told her about a new restaurant near her home that would soon need a chef. She applied, and she received a job offer before the restaurant started a formal search.
- Sometimes parents can help. A recent law school graduate was having difficulty finding a job. During dinner with friends, his parents mentioned that their son was looking for work. As it happened, their friends' nephew was a lawyer in the process of expanding his business. Introductions were made, and a couple of weeks later, the young graduate was employed.

88. Are You Making Rookie Job-Hunting Mistakes?

As a result of working with a number of recent college graduates, I've noticed that their inexperience with the workplace affects their job search. Here are six rookie job-hunting mistakes and ways to avoid making them. (Some of them apply to experienced job seekers too.)

1. **Giving up.** One graduate couldn't find a position in her field, so she took a low-paying clerical job and stopped her search. It's fine to take temporary work, but don't throw in the towel. Spend time on your search, and give it your all. Some people make only a halfhearted effort when seeking employment, thereby missing out on potential opportunities. If you keep searching, you will increase your chances of landing the job you really want.

2. **Not doing your research on job hunting.** This may be the first time you are looking for professional employment. There is a lot of information readily available on the Internet. Reading about looking for work can suggest approaches for your own search.

3. **Eliminating yourself.** You may think you should not apply for a position unless you meet all the job requirements. Apply anyway. You still may be a good fit for the position—or you may be perfect for another opening at the same company.

4. **Having typos in your résumé or cover letter.** Typographical mistakes show that you are not paying attention to the details. And why would someone hire you if you mail out documents containing errors? Always have someone proofread your documents.

5. **Apologizing for your inexperience.** Avoid saying, "I'm sorry, I have never done that." Emphasize what you *have* done.

6. **Not having a coach.** A coach keeps you focused on your search. You report to your coach regularly about your activities, and you discuss additional opportunities to explore. You can hire a coach or ask someone you know—preferably a trusted, professional adult—to be your coach.

POINT TO PONDER

One recent graduate with a 3.8 grade point average (GPA) from an excellent university wanted a coach to help him during his job search. He said, "I want every possible advantage when I start looking for a position." He had an attractive offer within a month.

89. I Got the Interview. Now What?

A recent graduate interviewed for a position, but the work described wasn't exactly what he wanted. When asked by the interviewer what he thought of the opportunity, the graduate replied, "It wouldn't be my first choice."

Not surprisingly, he didn't get the job offer, and he stayed unemployed.

POINT TO PONDER

Your résumé may have gotten you the interview, but how you handle yourself during the interview will get you the job.

You don't want to do anything that will make it easy for the hiring manager to move on to someone else. Here are suggestions to help job seekers of all ages alleviate the jitters associated with interviewing:

1. **Prepare meaningful discussion points.** Know "the stories of your life." Think of positive, specific examples ahead of time that demonstrate your competency, such as how you handled rude customers or difficult employees, and use these illustrations when you answer questions.

2. **Practice interviewing with a colleague or friend.** You will learn where you stumble and whether you use *like* or *um*. Be open to the feedback that you are given. Anticipate the tough questions, and know how you will answer them.

3. **Do your research.** Visit the company's website, and like them if they have a Facebook page. Talk to people who work there. Your LinkedIn contacts may help you identify people who work or have worked at the company. They may be able to put in a good word

for you or provide valuable information about the company. A family friend was interviewing at a company where one of my relatives worked. My relative gave the friend some great insights into the company's culture. Her suggestions proved helpful in the interviewing process. The friend got the job!

4. **Don't dress inappropriately.** After interviewing a number of people at a job fair, the consultant said she wouldn't hire any of them. All of the applicants were dressed too casually—they weren't dressed as if they were coming to work at her company. (See Etiquette 90, "Dressing for an Interview: Do You Look the Part?")

POINT TO PONDER

A candidate wore a shirt emblazoned with small teddy bears to an interview. He didn't get the job; the interviewers just kept talking about his shirt. Wearing ties or T-shirts with inappropriate sayings, pictures, or childish designs can hurt your professional image.

---

5. **Shake hands twice.** Believe it or not, one of the simplest things you can do to convey a sense of confidence and professionalism is to shake hands properly at the beginning of the interview and at the end. And shake hands with everyone in the room. (See Etiquette 7, "The Thumb Joint Connects to the . . . Thumb Joint," for more information on the handshake.)

6. **Be enthusiastic.** Don't be nonchalant about the position. Many candidates have good job skills, but they seem passive during the interview. You need to be engaging. Don't slouch, and avoid nervous gestures such as hair-twirling. Look the interviewer in the eye, and smile during the interview. Even if the job is not your first choice, you want to come across as someone who is interested in the position and the company.

7. **Answer the questions clearly and concisely.** You have prepared, and you have practiced. You are ready! Speak with conviction. Answer the questions, and don't overtalk. If you act as though

you are confident, others will perceive you that way (even if that's not how you feel on the inside).

8. **Have questions to ask.** Usually, you will be asked at the end of the interview if you have any questions for the interviewer. Prepare a couple of questions ahead of time and ask them. It shows your interest in the position. Listed below are some samples that you can adapt to your situations:

- "What brought you to this company?"

- "How do you see my skill set matching up with the position?"

- "What would you consider key success factors for this job?"

- "What do you like about working here?"

9. **Send thank you notes.** Write to each of the people who interviewed you. An emailed thank you note is acceptable in most situations. It's one way to set yourself apart from other applicants. Many human resources people reduce the pile of applications by weeding out job seekers who didn't send a thank you note. (See Etiquette 17, "Thank You Notes Do Matter.")

10. **Learn from each interview.** What worked? What can you improve upon? Review the questions you were asked. How did you answer them? How will you answer them in the future?

Q. *I just had a phone interview, and I was very nervous. I feel like I rambled a bit much and did not get the points across that properly represented me. What are your thoughts about addressing this in my thank you letter?*

A. It is possible that you are just being hard on yourself. You may not have been as unfocused as you thought. And even if you were, I would not mention that you felt like you rambled. If you say that, you will be emphasizing it. I would just reiterate your strengths in your thank you note.

---

90. Dressing for an Interview:
Do You Look the Part?

After arriving at work one morning, a young woman was surprised to find out that her interview for a new position inside her company had been scheduled for that afternoon. She panicked at first, as she wasn't dressed for an interview. But after some quick thinking, she took an early lunch and went to the nearby mall to buy a suit and a pair of shoes. She left the store wearing her new outfit, and then she felt ready for the interview.

A client shared the above story with me, and her resourcefulness made my day! What you wear to an interview does matter. It is part of the first impression you make on others. My niece (who is always well dressed) interviewed for a job and received this feedback from the hiring manager: "As soon as I saw you, I knew I would hire you. You looked the part."

Here are some suggestions so you, too, can "look the part":

1. **Choose something that you like to wear.** You want to feel good in your clothes. If you are concerned about your selection, it will distract you during the interview. Yes, I know you are comfortable in sweats and a T-shirt, but you know that is not the type of clothing that I am talking about.

2. **Have your interview clothes ready at all times.** Always be prepared. You do not want to find out on the eve of an interview that you have nothing to wear or that your clothes are at the cleaners. Anything you wear should be clean and pressed. Interviews can be scheduled with a very short lead time, and you always want to have something appropriate to wear.

3. **Make sure your clothes fit**. If your clothes are too big or too small, they are not going to look good. They also need to fit without overemphasizing your body. You want people to focus on what you are saying, not on your curves. Ensuring a proper fit applies to everything you are wearing. One interviewer said he was distracted by a man's short tie.

4. **Should you wear a suit**? This question is asked often in today's business casual work environment. Consider the following four points as you make a decision:

   - **Were you told what to wear?** If so, follow those guidelines. Also, if possible ask someone for guidance, such as a recruiter or a contact at the company.

   - **Consider the type of company.** Technology firms may be more casual in their dress than banking and finance companies.

   - **Consider the level of the position.** The higher the position, the more likely you will want to wear a suit. A young woman I coached interviewed at a public relations firm. Since it was for a vice president's position, she wore a suit—and got the job.

   - **When in doubt, wear a suit.** Companies know that you're dressing to impress. Even if you won't be wearing a suit for your job, you may still consider wearing one for the interview. When one young man interviewed for a position at an information technology company, he wore a suit. He got the job—and now he can wear jeans and sneakers to work.

5. **Pay attention to the little things**. One recruiter told me the first thing he notices about a candidate is his or her shoes. Make sure your shoes are polished and in good condition. Women's long red nails with designs on them or men's socks that allow skin to show when they cross their legs can also become distractions.

91. Talking Your Way to Success: Presentation Tips

Barbara, I need a few quick tips to make sure I appear confident and credible when I speak to our board next week.

The above voice mail message was left by a vice president for human resources who often sent her employees to my classes but hadn't had the time to come herself. Four items came to mind immediately. They are straightforward suggestions, and they can be very effective for anyone making a presentation:

1. **Practice out loud.** You want to hear how your presentation sounds. Saying it in your head isn't good enough. Is it structured logically? Are you using transitions between points? Are the stories complete? Does the presentation make sense? Hearing the speech as your audience will hear it will help to clarify what you need to work on.

2. **Look at people.** Presenters sometimes get nervous and tend to avoid looking at the people they are addressing. Keep in mind that when you make eye contact with members of your audience, you appear confident and in control of the presentation *and* your audience. And make sure you look at everyone. People have a tendency to look only at the people who smile at them (and we do love these people!). Try instead to look at everyone in the audience because you don't want to miss connecting with anyone.

3. **Remember the *92 percent rule*.** This basic principle of mine reminds people that they don't have to be perfect. *Whew. Take the pressure off!* You don't want to let a small flaw ruin—in your mind—an otherwise good presentation. You can end up focusing on the error, which can cause you to make more mistakes. Being a little

less than perfect, 92 percent, means you are still very effective—in most classes, that would earn you an A. When you relieve yourself of the pressure to be perfect, you may be surprised at how successful you are.

4. **Manage the questions.** At the beginning of your talk, let people know when you will take questions. You often can direct people to ask questions on a specific topic by saying, "What questions do you have about X?" When someone asks a question, repeat it before you answer, not only so that the audience can hear it clearly but also to give you a few seconds to compose your thoughts. You also can rephrase the question to eliminate any negativity. When it's time to conclude the question period, let the audience know by saying, "I have time for one more question."

POINT TO PONDER

An audience doesn't automatically know you are nervous. If you are not verbally or nonverbally conveying your nervousness, the audience will never know. And if the audience doesn't know, why waste your energy being nervous? Interesting concept . . . and it has helped a lot of people overcome their nervousness.

92. Three Things *Not* to Say in a Presentation

In some of my recent presentation skills seminars, I have noticed that many participants start their presentations with self-deprecating statements. These comments belittle the speaker or his or her speech, and they can cause the audience to run for the exits, at least metaphorically.

Why would speakers do that to themselves?

Some presenters make these kinds of comments because they feel insecure about their topic or their public-speaking ability. Others aren't even aware that they are making these overly modest remarks.

Find out whether you have a tendency to be self-deprecating. Record your presentation, and get feedback from others. Are you using any of the following belittling comments?

- **"I hope I don't bore you, but I am going to talk about . . ."** When you say "bored," the audience immediately expects to be bored. You need to appear excited about your topic, whether you are or not.

- **"I know you didn't come here to hear me."** You are undervaluing yourself. You don't need to say this.

- **"I haven't had a lot of time to prepare."** Why would an audience want to listen to someone who is unprepared? Instead, express yourself positively and say something like, "I have quickly put together some suggestions for . . . ."

The good news is that once people realize they are being self-deprecating, with a little practice they can eliminate those remarks from their presentations.

93. Dread Presentations?
Let's Change That!

During a class on presentation skills, one of the participants declared that if she wasn't passionate about the topic, she couldn't do a good job.

I regularly hear that rationale for not wanting to make a presentation. But I don't buy it.

I believe that although you may not always be passionate about your topic, you *can* always be passionate about the presentation.

Really? What does that mean? It means that you hone your presentation skills so that when you give a presentation, regardless of your topic, you know how to do the following:

- Organize your presentation for impact

- Use your posture, eye contact, gestures, and word choices to convey confidence

- Answer questions effectively to build your credibility

- Use your voice to command attention

- Dress for the presentation in a way that enhances your professionalism

When you do these things, you are building your reputation in front of your audience.

Why wouldn't you be passionate about that?

94. Difficult Audience?
Try These Suggestions

Most audiences want you to do well. Occasionally, however, you may encounter people who do not want to be in your audience or who have strong, sometimes negative, opinions about your topic.

Practice these suggestions to help win over any audience:

- **Know your audience.** Learn as much as you can about your audience before your presentation. What do they already know about your topic? What more do they want to know? If you address your participants' needs and concerns, they are more likely to listen and less likely to object to your comments.

POINT TO PONDER

You can find out about your audience by talking with the person who organized your talk or with people who have presented previously to that particular audience. You can also learn a lot by mingling with audience members before the presentation.

- **Meet the participants.** When you can, go up to people, shake hands, introduce yourself, and welcome these individuals to the presentation. This rapport building helps people connect with you, and they are then less likely to give you a hard time.

- **Establish credibility.** Make sure the audience knows why you are qualified to talk about the subject. If you are not introduced, make sure you give a self-introduction at the beginning of your presentation. And this is *not* the time to be modest. The more knowledgeable the audience thinks you are, the less likely they are to challenge you.

- **Project confidence whether you feel it or not.** Don't show or tell the audience that you are uncomfortable. Look people in the eye. Stand when you can. Dress for the presentation. And speak loudly enough to be heard.

- **Handle the individual difficult person.** If the audience likes you but one person starts to give you a tough time, often another audience member will shut him or her down. I still remember an incident years ago when one man kept questioning my suggestions. Eventually, another man, a few rows behind him, called out, "Oh, sit down and shut up. I wouldn't want to work for you." And the heckler promptly sat.

  You also could say to the person hassling you, "I know that you and I have different opinions. Let's get together after the program and discuss them. I have a lot to cover right now." You would then subtly angle your body away from him and continue your talk.

- **Anticipate any objections people may have, and know how you will respond.** Prepare ahead of time for every possible negative, harsh comment or question you can imagine. Try not to be caught off guard.

95. Help! Someone Is Sleeping During My Talk!

What do you do when someone falls asleep during your presentation?

My first thought after being asked this question during a recent presentation skills seminar was to recall the scene in the movie *Larry Crowne*, where Julia Roberts throws an eraser at her sleeping student.

My second thought was, "You can't do that in the business world!" However, since I have been asked about sleeping or daydreaming participants a number of times over the last few years, here are some alternative suggestions:

1. **Don't take it personally; sometimes people just need to sleep.** Some years ago, I noticed a woman sleeping in the first row of my seminar. I admit that it was a little unnerving. But she came up to me at break and said, "I am loving your seminar, but I had a migraine this morning and took my medicine, and I know at times it makes me drowsy. But I'm learning so much that I want to stay, and I wanted you to know that." I responded with a gracious, and heartfelt, "Thank you!"

2. **Ask yourself: Are you making it too easy for people to doze off?** Are you speaking in a monotone? Too softly? Is the room too hot? Too dark? Are your slides difficult to read? If any of these scenarios describes your presentation, some of your audience may fall asleep.

3. **Have you added any stories?** In a presentation, don't just deliver a collection of related data. Adding stories that support your information can enliven your presentation and keep your audience's attention. To highlight the importance of the speaker's making eye

contact with the audience, I often tell the story of a judge who instructed a witness to remove his dark glasses so the jury could see his eyes. (See the "Tell Tales: Bring Your Presentation to Life" box for more information on stories.)

4. **Walk around or near the sleeper.** When you walk around your room, your activity may wake the person. Sometimes a participant sitting next to the dozing person will tap the sleeper.

5. **Call a break, or have the group do an exercise.** These options are usually possible during an informal presentation. Make sure you talk to the sleeper during this time to engage him or her.

6. **Ask the person a question.** This can be risky, and you need to do this very cautiously because you do not want to put someone on the spot. But if a person is only nodding off momentarily or daydreaming, you may want to try it. Say the person's name and then ask a question or ask for a comment, but take care to restate the topic—for example, "Tom, you are the expert on budgeting. Would you please add your comments on _____?"

TELL TALES: BRING YOUR PRESENTATION TO LIFE

When discussing a specific point, concept, product, or service, tell a story about someone's proving your point or benefiting from your service. Your audience will remember the story and as a result your presentation.

Very few of my participants ever forget my story of going to the bathroom with my microphone on. I use it to illustrate the point that it's not what happens to you that matters. It is how you handle what happens to you.

Follow these guidelines to add stories—and power—to your presentations:

- Make sure your story involves a person (or an animal), and it is relevant to your point.
- Don't use people's names unless you have their approval or they are public figures.
- Never lie—but you can embellish for dramatic effect. Unfortunately,

my cordless microphone story has not been embellished!

- Create a story file. When you experience something or read about someone you think might make a good story, file it away—either in an electronic file or in an old-fashioned manila folder. Either way, when you start to prepare a presentation, go to your file for material.
- Be cautious with humor. Humor can add a lot to your story, but it can also bomb badly.
- Don't put anyone down or criticize someone.

96. Don't Present Like, You Know, Um, a Young Person

How do we appear experienced and mature, when we're not?

The above question was asked recently by a young man as I was giving feedback to a group of new hires during a sales presentation class. He and the other participants in the class were bright, talented individuals, but they needed to play down their youthful demeanor. Their customers, high-net-worth individuals, wanted to buy from sources who presented themselves as credible and mature.

I suggested that they eliminate discounting, immature mannerisms from their sales pitches to appear more self-assured and confident. Seasoned professionals also can check their presentations against this list.

Here are the top 10 things to avoid when making a sales presentation:

1. **Don't use the words *hope* and *hopefully*.** You don't want to appear unsure. A number of the presenters had said "We hope you will choose us" and "Hopefully, we can work together." Instead, the presenters should have acted confidently and said, "We look forward to working with you."

2. **Never use "You guys" when referencing audience members.** Do I really need to explain this one? It's a young person's language, and it's too casual.

3. **Don't introduce yourself with your first name only.** If you are not introduced before you make your presentation, give both your first and last names when introducing yourself. Your full name gives you more standing.

4. **Avoid the phrase *to be honest with you*.** Customers want to believe that you are *always* honest with them. (See Etiquette 27, "The Do-Not-Say List," for more phrases to avoid.)

5. **Eliminate the monotone voice.** You need to be enthusiastic, without going overboard. One presenter said, "We're excited about the turnaround at our firm," but she didn't sound as though she believed it. Occasionally, emphasize keywords to animate your sentences.

6. **Don't play with things.** Don't play with your pen or a rubber band or anything else when speaking to others. This distracting mannerism conveys nervousness. Keep your hands empty. Men, don't play with change in your pockets; and women, don't twirl your hair. One young woman kept putting a strand of her long hair into her mouth! You want to appear self-assured.

7. **Don't dress like a kid.** Your attire can help you appear as a credible, successful person. And appearance matters in the business world. If you look like you just got out of bed, you won't appear to be taking your customers' business seriously. Dress to impress your customers.

8. **Don't use filler words.** If your audience is counting the number of *um*'s in your talk, they are not listening to you. Plus, filler words make you appear young, nervous, and unprepared.

9. **Avoid *I think* or *we think*.** When you say "I think," you are telling the audience that you don't know. One presenter said, "We think we are a much stronger company today." Speak with conviction and say, "We are a much stronger company today."

10. **Do your homework.** You may not have been with your company for five years, or even one year, but you can learn about its recent history. Being familiar with your company's projects, policies, successes, and failures will bolster your credibility and allow you to talk with confidence to your current clients.

97. It May Be Funny, but It's Not Assertive

A colleague wanted to know my opinion about a young woman who quit her job after she overheard her boss make a disparaging remark about her.

She had resigned, rather creatively, by sending an email to her boss and her 22 coworkers that contained a series of photographs where she held a dry eraser board with a different comment explaining her reasons for resigning.

The disparaging remark was given as a reason in one of the photographs. In another, she said that working with her boss had been a special form of hell. In others, she said that the boss had a temper and bad breath and he spent a lot of time on the Internet doing non-work-related activities.

Many people, including my colleague, thought she was very clever in her resignation approach.

I agree she was clever . . . but also passive. She failed to act in her own best interest. She never told her boss at the time, or subsequently, that she was offended by his comment. She simply quit a good job without having another one.

Learning to say "I'm offended by your comment" can be difficult. Yet using this assertive sentence provides the possibility of eliminating bad behavior in others, improving your relationships, and feeling good about yourself.

Had she told her boss she was offended, it is feasible that he might have apologized. He may have stopped making negative comments about her, or he may have viewed her differently because she confronted him directly. Her working relationship with him may have improved.

Of course, it is also possible that nothing she might have said would have made a difference. But, as I discuss in my book *The Power of Positive Confrontation*, what did she have to lose by trying? Unfortunately, she'll never know. She quit her job before she could find out.

Q. *My coworker is continually chatting with me throughout the workday. Can I approach my boss and ask to move to another cube?*

A. Before you contact the boss, you should talk to your coworker. Strange as it may sound, she may not even realize she is annoying you, especially since it appears you are chatting with her.

The next time she talks too much, speak up and be assertive with her. Many people fear hurting others' feelings, and they won't tell coworkers, friends, boyfriends, or others that what they are doing is bothering them. But there is another way to handle these situations. Speak calmly and politely, and say something like, "Let me talk to you later. I have to get this work done." If she continues to talk, you can keep repeating: "You know, Jen, I really need to get work done. Let's talk later." Or "Let's talk at lunch." I would then make a point of chatting with her at lunch or at the end of the day.

---

98. Assert Yourself:
Learn to Speak Up at Meetings

Have you ever left a meeting or conference thinking, "I wish I had said something"?

You are not alone. People often come up to me and confess that they are hesitant to speak up at meetings. Others mention that when they do say something, no one responds. Check your behavior against this list of nine key assertiveness points to make sure your voice is heard:

1. **Do you understand the consequences of not speaking up?** You want your bosses, colleagues, and customers to view you as competent and credible. If you don't speak up, they don't know what you know, and you can become overlooked and irrelevant.

2. **Do you prepare ahead of time?** It is easier to say something when you have practiced. Spend some time thinking about the meeting and what may be discussed. Familiarize yourself with what you want to say so that you can say it with confidence when the topic comes up. (If the topic doesn't come up, this exercise has not been wasted; you will be ready for the next meeting.)

3. **Do you speak early?** The longer you wait to give your opinion, the harder it will be to speak up. Make a comment or ask a question near the beginning of the meeting.

4. **Do you make your point without asking permission?** Do you say, "May I make a point?" When you ask permission, it's easy for others to think, "No." Either say "I have a point" or simply speak out with your comments.

5. **Do you put yourself down?** Don't start your comments with "It's only my opinion" or similar statements. And don't conclude with "I don't know. What do you think?" If you discount yourself, it's easy for others to discount you as well.

6. **Do you speak loudly enough to be heard?** If you speak softly, your comments may not register with others. Practice increasing your volume. Initially, you may feel that you are shouting, but the chances are that you are finally speaking loudly enough to be heard. (Additional information on volume can be found in Etiquette 26, "Speak Up! We Can't Hear You.")

7. **Do you stand up when you can?** If there is a valid reason for you to stand when you make your presentation—other presenters have stood, for instance, or the meeting is more formal—you should do so. The extra height gives you power because the meeting participants have to look up at you. If you can't stand, make sure you position yourself on the same level as others.

8. **Do you know how to interrupt?** Yes, I know, interrupting is generally frowned upon. Yet, in some situations, if you don't interrupt, you won't get to speak. The easiest way to interrupt is when the other person takes a breath. You then speak up quickly, acknowledge what the person said, and add your thoughts.

9. **Do you avoid giving too much detail?** If you belabor your points, people tune out. Say what you need to say in as few words as necessary.

TRY THIS SUGGESTION

Use prompts. One young man who is inclined to go off on a lot of tangents during discussions puts "LCD" at the top of his papers before going to a meeting so he remembers to give "less conversational detail."

---

99. Ending the Never-Ending Discussion

When I teach my conflict class, I am frequently asked: "When you have a difference of opinion with someone, how do you stop the endless, exasperating, back-and-forth exchange of positions?"

This situation often occurs when one person is trying to persuade the other of his or her viewpoint.

There isn't one perfect way to get out of this type of conversation, but outlined below are various options to try. Some of them contain comments that you can adapt to your situation. I have collected these examples over the last couple of years from listening to public figures and from conversations with participants in my seminars:

1. **Broaden the scope of the discussion.** *TODAY Show* anchor Matt Lauer did this successfully a few years ago during an interview with actor Tom Cruise when he said: "Let me take this [psychiatry discussion] more general because I think you and I can go around in circles on this for a while. And I respect your opinion." Lauer then asked Cruise a wide-ranging question.

2. **State that you won't participate in the disagreement.** Politely but powerfully let the other person know that you won't engage in the discussion. Recently, Philadelphia mayor Michael Nutter replied to a reporter's repeated question at a press conference: "I'm not getting into a back-and-forth. The answer is the answer."

3. **Use the broken-record approach.** With this technique, you state your position over and over, until the other person truly hears you. A seminar participant told me she did this with her coworker when she kept repeating, "I'm swamped. I'm unable to help you with this project." He finally said, "Oh, okay, I'll get someone else."

4. **Take a break.** You let the person know that you need time to think more about the topic and will get back to him or her later.

When you use any of those options, make sure that your voice is calm and steady. You want to appear assertive, not aggressive.

100. Smart Tips When Traveling for Business

A couple had some problems with the ticketing for a trip, and both were yelling and being rude to the ticket agent. The agent kept her cool and took care of their problems. After the couple left, the ticket agent next to her said, "Boy, they were really being nasty to you." The agent replied, "That's okay. They're going to London—their luggage is going to Bulgaria!"

There are lots of reasons to stay calm and exhibit good manners when traveling, as my favorite travel story above illustrates. You don't want your luggage going to Bulgaria.

I know that keeping your cool when traveling can be a challenge, especially since passengers are paying more and still enduring long lines, cancellations, and lost luggage. With atypical weather patterns on the increase—how many times in the last decade have we experienced a *storm of the century*?—delays, rerouting, and other disruptive occurrences are becoming commonplace in air travel.

Polite behavior cannot stop a storm, but it can make a bad situation easier to endure. Here are eight tips to help you be "travel smart":

1. **Be prepared for delays.** Take food and water with you. (Remember to buy water *after* you go through airport security, so that it won't be confiscated.) Have your necessities in your carry-on bag. Make sure your cell phone and all electronic devices are fully charged, and maybe carry a battery-powered emergency charger. Always have something to read, listen to, or watch. If you are prepared for the worst, you'll be less stressed and better able to handle any negative situation that may arise.

2. **Don't engage in any cursing, name-calling, or other rude behavior.** Do you really think that the person you just called all sorts of names

will want to help you? One ticket agent I heard about deliberately scheduled a foul-mouthed passenger for a four-hour wait when an earlier flight was available. Customer service people tell me that although they are required to help rude people, they will do as little as possible. If you are polite, they are more likely to go out of their way for you.

3. **Don't make threats.** In the post-9/11 world, threats are taken seriously. Don't joke around or try to intimidate people.

4. **Acknowledge the difficulty.** When talking to the customer service person who can potentially help you, acknowledging his or her challenges can go a long way in helping you connect. Simply say: "It looks like it has been a really tough day," or "It has been a difficult time, hasn't it?"

5. **Politely ask for what you want.** If you ask for what you want, and it's a reasonable request, you are more apt to get it. Saying "Any chance for a dinner coupon?" may very well produce one.

6. **Befriend other passengers.** It makes for a more pleasant trip when things get difficult. You will have a "we're in this together" mentality. As a bonus, people may share what they know. During one flight delay I experienced, a man with whom I had chatted earlier found out that the airline had opened a new line upstairs. Before he went upstairs, he came and told me.

7. **Be alert, but don't be a bully.** Pay attention to your surroundings. Additional customer service personnel may appear, and new lines may open up to process passenger requests. You need to be ready to move quickly—but it's not okay to push or shove.

8. **Don't announce your travel plans on your social-media sites.** There are numerous examples of people's homes being burglarized because they let their "friends" know they were away. A headline in the *New York Times* summed it up best: "Burglars Said to Have Picked Houses Based on Facebook Updates."

101. I Accept Your Quirks Because
You Accept Mine

I returned from a short vacation and decided to coin a new term—
pre-travel anxiety (PTA).

Let me explain.

My husband is a nervous traveler. For some unknown reason, his
PTA was particularly acute this trip. He packed two weeks before we
left, and he kept reminding me to do the same; he repeatedly asked me
to get our boarding passes days before we were able to do so; and he
had us leave for the airport at the crack of dawn for a 10 a.m. flight.
Consider that we live only 20 minutes from the airport and this was
a domestic flight!

I wanted to scream at times. But I took a deep breath, decided that
PTA was one of his quirks, and let it go.

"I accept your quirks because you accept mine" is a concept from
my assertiveness class.

You could find reasons to argue with people all day long. But no
one is perfect. And if you expect someone to be, you are bound to be
disappointed—and more likely to argue with the person as a result.

We all have our idiosyncrasies (I have some, but I won't tell you
what they are), and when you accept other people's differences, they're
more likely to accept yours.

Practicing this approach in business as well as in your personal
relationships will help you to reduce conflict in your life.

Conclusion

If you have read all 101 entries in this book, you should have an excellent grasp of business etiquette. But you need to put these suggestions into action. I don't expect you to remember everything—so keep the book handy, and review the entries that apply to your position or current concerns at any given time. This will have an impact on your career in the future.

For example, if you are unsure whether some piece of clothing is suitable for wearing to work, check out entry Etiquette 35, "Just the FACS, Madam: Business Clothing Essentials," to help you make a decision. If you are a bit anxious about a photo or comment you *really* want to post on your Facebook page, Etiquette 67, "Costly Mistakes with Tweets, Posts, and Requests," might persuade you not to do so. Or if you have to send an important email, follow the points in Etiquette 73, "Email Etiquette 1: Avoid Saying or Doing the Wrong Thing," to come across as a polished, confident professional.

I tell the participants at the end of my seminars that they have been given the skills, tools, and resources to make some changes in how they present themselves in the workplace—if they choose to do so. And I wish them well on that journey.

I wish you the same success.

Index

About the Authors

Barbara Pachter
Speaker, Author, and Coach

Barbara Pachter is an internationally renowned business etiquette and communications speaker, coach, and author. She has delivered more than 2,100 seminars throughout the world including the first-ever seminar for businesswomen in Kuwait. In 2010, *NJBiz* named her one of the Best 50 Women in Business in New Jersey. Pachter is also an adjunct faculty member in the School of Business at Rutgers University.

Her client list boasts many of today's most notable organizations, including Bayer HealthCare, Campbell Soup, Children's Hospital of Philadelphia, Chrysler, Cisco Systems, Cleveland Clinic, Con Edison, Ecolab, Educational Testing Services (ETS), Microsoft, Pfizer, TD Bank, and Wawa.

Pachter is the author of nine books including *When the Little Things Count . . . And They Always Count* and *The Power of Positive Confrontation*. Her books have been translated into 11 languages.

She is quoted regularly in newspapers and magazines, including the *Wall Street Journal*, the *New York Times*, *TIME Magazine*, and *O Magazine*, and she has appeared on ABC's *20/20*, *The TODAY Show*, and *The Early Show*. Her discussion on business etiquette appeared in the *Harvard Business Review*.

Pachter's areas of expertise include business etiquette, presentation skills, business writing, positive confrontation, business dress, assertive communication, career suggestions, and women in the workplace. She holds undergraduate and graduate degrees from the University of Michigan, and she has completed postgraduate studies in the Middle East and at Temple University. She is a former teacher of English as a second language (ESL).

Pachter can be contacted at Pachter & Associates, PO Box 3680, Cherry Hill, NJ 08034, USA, 856-751-6141; bpachter@pachter.com; www.pachter.com.

To connect with Pachter via social media:

- www.facebook.com/pachtertraining
- www.barbarapachtersblog.com
- www.linkedin.com/in/barbarapachter
- www.twitter.com/barbarapachter

Denise Cowie
Writer and Editor

Denise Cowie was born and raised in Australia, but she has lived most of her adult life as a journalist in the United States. She has worked for newspapers on three continents, including many years at the *Philadelphia Inquirer*, where her assignments included a range of editing roles as well as several years as a feature writer and columnist. Since leaving daily journalism in late 2005, she has added managing a nonprofit website for a consortium of public gardens to her résumé, as well as writing and editing for magazines, books, and websites.

Cowie serves on the board of several nonprofit organizations. She is a Fellow of the Garden Writers Association of North America, and she also has been a judge for that organization's national media awards.